Bright Moon, White Clouds

Bright Moon, White Clouds

Selected Poems of Li Po

EDITED AND TRANSLATED BY

J.P. Seaton

SHAMBHALA
Boston & London
2012

Shambhala Publications, Inc.
Horticultural Hall
300 Massachusetts Avenue
Boston, Massachusetts 02115
www.shambhala.com

9 8 7 6 5 4 3 2 1

First Edition
Printed in the United States of America

⊗ This edition is printed on acid-free paper that meets the
American National Standards Institute z39.48 Standard.
♻ Shambhala Publications makes every effort to print
on recycled paper. For more information please visit
www.shambhala.com.

Distributed in the United States by Random House, Inc., and in
Canada by Random House of Canada Ltd

LIBRARY OF CONGRESS CATALOGING-IN-PUBLICATION DATA

Li, Bai, 701–762.
[Poems. English. Selections]
Bright moon, white clouds: selected poems of Li Po / edited and
translated by J.P. Seaton.—1st ed.
p.   cm.
ISBN 978-1-59030-746-5 (pbk.: acid-free paper)
1. Li, Bai, 701–762—Translations into English. I. Seaton, Jerome
P. II. Title.
PL2671.A2 2012
895.1'13—dc23
2011035929

To Rosalie Katherine Paradiso Seaton

Contents

PART FOUR

PART FIVE

Bright Moon, White Clouds

Introduction

THIS IS A BOOK OF POEMS IN TRANSLATION. The poems are what we call immortal, as is the author, Li Po, the Chinese poet of the eighth century of the common era. But this book is not a celebration of any kind of "immortality" at all. Let me call it a wake, instead, and invite you to come join me in a joyous celebration of this complicated man's life's work.

Li Po was born in 701. He was not born ten feet tall, but legend has it that he may have grown to be. In the borderlands of China's desert Northeast, somewhere in the modern-day province of Kan-su, many religions still competed, and the expansions of Muhammad's new dispensation accounted for migrations into China, and those new migrants brought still more religions. Thus we can't be too surprised to learn that Li Po was, in one story, miraculously conceived and delivered by the spirit of the planet known in China as T'ai-po, the morning star, *our* planet Venus. Li Po is indeed also known as Li T'ai-po. Only a little more down to earth, maybe, was Li Po's own claim. Our poet chose to regard himself as a descendant of an ancestor of the Imperial family of T'ang China, another man named Li. That man was Li Er, also known as Li Tan, or more commonly as Lao Tzu, the "old philosopher." In a multilevel pun, Lao Tzu means the "old baby." Unlike his "descendant" Li Po, the old philosopher who was the founder of the Li family line as well as the author of the book called the *Lao Tzu* was supposed to have been born already having attained, in utero, the age of seventy: thus the "old baby," one who combines the wisdom of age with the directness and simplicity of the speechless child. Lao Tzu, under compulsion, wrote all his wisdom into a single book of fewer than five thousand words, which came to be known as the *Tao Te Ching*, or *Classic of the Way and Its Power*. All this biographical information about the man called Lao Tzu might seem out of place if it were not for the fact that Li Po is regarded today, and has been regarded for at least a thousand years, rightly or wrongly, as the leading poetic proponent of Lao Tzu's Tao, his Way, or his "philosophy." In a career move not uncommon in his time, as bizarrely "un-Taoist" as it might seem to modern lovers of Taoism, he even took a *degree* in it. Maybe more to the point in the mind of *his* public, to the people who made him a legend alive and a god beyond death, he drank, sang, and made love to the music of the *Tao Te Ching*.

That the Imperial family also shared his family name was a convenience in the baby's later life: Li was an extremely common surname in the T'ang, and is the most common among all Chinese in the twenty-first century C.E. Countless people claimed to be relations of royalty, few with the good-natured tenacity and apparent success of Li Po.

If we refuse to accept *legends* about Li Po's birth and early life, we can still know much more than less than nothing. It's very likely that Li Po was born in the outer reaches of the Empire, son of a "no one," or of a convict in exile, or of a minor official with a real, if minimal, claim to relationship to the Imperial family of China's greatest empire, the T'ang (618–905 C.E.). The content of his early education makes it seem *possible* that he was raised, or educated at least, in a Taoist monastery. Or maybe the teenager, a physical giant by *all* accounts, took refuge in such a place, or even with a single monk, when an abortive career as a Robin Hood–style Chinese knight-errant went into a downward spiral in spite of his eight-foot stature (which we can correct to six foot eight because of the difference in kings' foot sizes in England post-1066 and China ca. 716

C.E.). Less likely-seeming than the swordsman legend (which Li Po himself liked to promote) is the story that he learned to be a bird trainer from another Master, and, since an affinity with wild animals (as Saint Francis had with the birds) is considered a mark of spiritual purity, he was offered a government job along with his Master.

If we are limited to the factual, we can't really know much for certain about the great Li Po. For the man universally regarded as one of China's two greatest poets, only a few paragraphs regarding his biography are preserved in the official history of the T'ang. But if there is little in the official histories, there is much in legend, and though some of it is nearly mythic in tone, most is so consistent, so constructive of a *reasonable* story, that I'm quite happy to offer a tale mixed from fact, fiction, and the desires of the popular imagination.

Another, more likely path to success may have been China's meritocratic one. T'ang's civil service examinations filled official positions in the central government—positions of real power—on the basis of merit rather than by blood relationship to the autocrat, king or emperor. These examinations began with the Chinese around 100 B.C.E., in the former Han dynasty, and flourished by the T'ang. Both the Jesuits and their friend Voltaire recommended such a system for Europe in the eighteenth century C.E. as a safety valve for Europe's ossified social structure, soon to be overthrown by waves of aristocratic blood. In the United States, civil service examinations were not begun until 1885.

The Chinese civil service examinations expanded slowly. But in the pivotal period, the golden age that was the T'ang, they were strongly bolstered by the government of Empress Wu, who made herself ruler, and were wisely extended by her successor, Li Po's Emperor, Hsuan Tsung, who reigned from 712 to 756 C.E. and is usually known, by virtue of his many very real accomplishments, as Ming Huang, or the "Brilliant Emperor."

Extremely important for Li Po's education, and eventual blossoming as a poet, was the fact that the sponsors of young men who did well in the examinations were themselves highly rewarded by the government, with both prestige and material gifts. Thus, whatever legends may say, Li Po was most likely curried and nurtured from an early age by *some* wise elder because of his obvious talent. If communicating with birds was a trick worthy of employment (though certainly not as a government official, whatever the popular legends imply), writing fine verse and classical prose as a teenager identified him as a potential leader, and certainly marked his sponsor as worthy of high reward as well.

The highest of the high in the civil service examinations, the *chin shih* exam, was *based entirely on the ability to write regulated verse*. The subject of the exam's poem was government, sometimes even current policy, and the "trick" was to be able to write one's answer in an extremely difficult style of verse called *lu shih*, or regulated verse, and in a language so loaded with allusion as to be practically in code. The winner was often a man already able to step into a leadership role at the highest level. Winners of the meritocratic prize at lower levels had already been freed of taxes and government tax labor for life, and could never again be subject to corporal punishment. Many men (of course, no women need apply) who passed the *chin shih* level were indeed given upper-echelon government appointments, and as a perk, they were generally allied by marriage to upper-crust families.

Everywhere in China, not just the young men but everyone around them knew all this. Even in a class society just beginning to see change, men of the middle and even the lower classes, and many among their wives, who were more educated than you'd expect, were starting to be greatly affected by the meritocratic ideas inherent in the examination system.

As a result of the almost incredible rewards attached to passing even the lower levels of the exams, wealthy families not seldom went so far as to adopt promising students, young people with the intellectual gifts and drive for both sheer hard work and creativity, specifically the type of poetic creativity that Li Po demonstrated. At any rate, sometime between the ages of five and twenty, Li Po discovered poetry, or poetry discovered him. Certainly by the time he was twenty-five he had mastered all the Classical knowledge that made up the core of the lower exams, and he was also a talented poet with a growing skill. There could be a million reasons why Li Po, unlike almost every one of the men regarded by contemporaries as nearly his equals as poets, failed to even take the exams. Maybe he realized that they were, in his prime, corrupt; maybe he realized that as a basically self-educated man he had little chance in the very specialized competitions. Maybe he was too busy, or asleep in a tavern down some alley. However, the examinations were almost certainly a part of the motivation for his studies at an early age.

At any rate, in the fullness of time, it came to pass that the young Li Po made an interesting trip across the hard road in Shu (see the poem on page 134) and an exciting Yang-tse voyage (as perhaps seen in the poem on page 136, which describes, if not this first trip, one along the same river route, the Long River, a trip that, as the description makes clear, would never have grown routine). So Li Po appeared in various points east. Once there, he began the perhaps demeaning process of currying favor for himself and his poetry among people who could *help* either or both. Eventually, on the strength of his "expectations," he married "well" and moved in with his wife's family. But after two children, no job for him, and a lot of drunken poetizing, she left him, and he was obviously no longer welcome at the in-laws' place. This didn't slow him down much, with so many "cousins" out there just waiting to put on display such a famous "guest."

In the 730s the very first thing a man could do to advance himself was to claim, as Li Po claimed, a drop or two of Imperial family blood in his veins. So, after this first of three divorces, lots of folks who also claimed to be related to the Imperial family, on the flimsy grounds that they were Lis themselves, received the visiting card of a certain Mr. Li, ostensibly their Imperial cousin. Many seem to have accepted it, and to have invited him to visit. It helped that *this* Mr. Li *clearly* was extraordinarily talented, and that he had a growing reputation as a *very* interesting young fellow.

Toward the end of this first great period of wandering, he "published" what was supposed to represent private letters recording an argument between himself and a highly renowned Taoist Master named Ssu-ma Ch'eng-cheng (655–735), in which Li Po had thrown a lot of insults at the Master. It was a pretty daring thing to do. Master Ssu-ma had among his credits the training of— as well as the administering of the examination on the contents of the *Tao Te Ching* to—another young man surnamed Li, a Mr. Li who was also known as the Emperor of China, Hsuan Tsung. The old man Ssu-ma Ch'eng-cheng had deeply offended Li Po, and many young Taoists in training like him, by *advising against drinking as a part of a serious mystical Taoist Path.* Li Po seems to have held something like a Timothy Leary position regarding alcohol as a chemical door. What was the difference between Taoism and Buddhism, he and his rowdy young friends may well have asked, if a Taoist had to teetotal like a Buddhist monk? What, indeed?

More study followed, ostensibly of Taoist alchemy, but certainly mainly of the practical applications of alcohol. There is an interesting suggestion in one of Li Po's acknowledged masterpieces, the third of the four poems under the heading "Drinking Alone under the Moon," that might be taken as a serious thought about the alchemy of alcohol, which is, after all, a psychoactive or even a theogenic substance, created by human transmutation of grains using our lowly "yeast," which is in fact a metaphor for the magical alchemical element *yeast*.

In this period he was attached to a group of young friends from the Shantung area whose companionship helped to bring him through the last remaining years before he met the man who was to mastermind his conquest of the Capital. That man, known as Wu Yun (his religious name), now controlled a resurgence in the popularity of Taoism as the socially and ideologically acceptable way of thought on the streets of the dynastic Capital, Ch'ang-an. Wu Yun had once failed the examination for the *chin shih* degree but had reestablished himself as something of a focal point of the rebirth of Taoism as the state ideology, the intellectual justification for legitimate sovereignty and political power. And it was under his auspices that Li Po in 742 at last made it to the Capital, almost certainly as a pawn in a political plot hatched by Wu Yun and the high official Ho Chih-chang. There may or may not have been a group of prominent "co-conspirators," including, just perhaps, a few of the aristocrats and famous artists celebrated by Tu Fu in his famous poem "Eight Immortals of the Winecup." According to Arthur Waley, in his biography of Li Po, only three people—Ho Chih-chang, Li Po himself, and Ts'ui Tsung-chih, one of Li's last best friends—are attested, during the T'ang, as members of this "group of eight," by anyone besides Tu Fu. At least two of them were either too young or too old to have been members. Tu Fu's "history" is part of Li Po's legend.

Li Po's job, if he should choose to accept it (and why would he not?), was *simply* to capture the Emperor's ear. The Emperor was, to put it mildly, a poetry lover, and Li Po would supplant his current favorite poet. But how much of the plan for a bloodless coup do you give to a graying wild boy? I believe this situation, as it stood on Li Po's arrival in the Capital, was in itself a fine argument in favor of the transparency of Li Po's good nature. He might be a conscious manipulator of little friends and great patrons, but Wu Yun, the Confucian turned Taoist Master, and Ho Chih-chang, by all accounts a *good man*, if an obviously eccentric character, had found, in Li Po's poetry and in his conversation, a man who *believed* in the absolute Taoist and Confucian requirement of fundamental honesty, of sincerity, and of loyalty—loyalty not to a *man*, not even "the One Man," "the Orphan," as the Emperor was called, but to a *principle*, the principle stated most clearly in its commonsense construction: "The Emperor is the Father and the Mother of the People."

According to Confucius's principle of Rectification of Names, when or if one behaves in accord with his title, whether it is Father or Emperor, justly if severely controlling the behavior of his "children," *while loving and nurturing them with equal attention,* he deserves in return the absolute devotion of his family or his government servants. They will behave as loving children behave toward their loving parents. If, however, the Father/Emperor deviates from his duty, he is *no longer* the Father/Emperor; *he has become a mere tyrant,* and loyalty to a tyrant is not required—in fact, it's not acceptable. This formulation is one of Confucius's great contributions to the Chinese idea of government, and it penetrated both Taoist and Buddhist political thought. I believe Wu Yun and Mr. Ho found these ideals in Li Po: he was a pampered celebrity, younger than his years, naive, perhaps, but he was also a romantic and an idealist. At any rate, it appears that as he imagined moving ever closer to the ear of the

One Man, he became more and more conscious of the duty conferred on him by the *gift of talent*, the duty at least to attempt to speak up, to speak out, for the people, because the government was corrupt and the onetime Brilliant Emperor was, probably in spite of himself, becoming a mere tyrant.

As we've seen, Li Po was a legend even before he came down through the rapids of the three gorges for the first time. Very quickly he was a notorious celebrity, and of course for twenty years he didn't mind. His celebrity brought him to the attention of the people who would eventually bring him to the Capital, and it also served as the seed around which his legends would grow into strings of crystal beads reflecting the Tai-po planet, brightest light in the morning sky, reflecting from their every facet.

But the legends also brought the true information, the *fact*, that he was addicted to the cup, ergo unstable—a "Mountain Lord," to put it in his own figure, in a poem where marketplace apes are made drunk by the local rowdies, with Li Po in the lead. Yes, he was a "Mountain Lord" at best. In one version of his first presentation to the Emperor as a new talent in the Capital, his own beloved Ho Chih-chang himself, perhaps covering himself *and* Li Po, in case the pawn proved unplayably wild, is said to have warned the Emperor of Li Po's reliance on "the thing in the cup," even as he presented him with a sample of the poet's work.

And so, rather than into some substantive political position as he may have naively expected, he was appointed "only" to the Hanlin Academy. It was a position any other man would have gloried in, and one that did give his work a chance to be seen very often by the Emperor. But instead of working assiduously toward that end, the drunken poet set about justifying everyone's opinion of his instability, while apparently continuing to entertain delusions of worldly influence. Perhaps his handlers even still felt that he had the power to remove the scales from the Emperor's eyes, to open the hard-eyed gaze of his early years as "the Brilliant Emperor" so that he might be brought, be it ever so painfully, to see that his beloved Yang Kuei-fei and her trusted but untrustworthy relatives, as well as his own prime minister, the able but corrupt Li Lin-fu, were very likely all conniving to overthrow him, or at least slowly displacing his power to govern, as they led him to devote himself ever more blindly to the joys of the harem.

Li Po's own poems tell us that on his first day on a Ch'ang-an avenue, Ho Chih-chang approached him, drawing a crowd, and announced in his loudest voice, much exercised at court, that the man before him was a "Banished Immortal," truly a celestial lord who'd been banished to earth by the gods for some unspecified length of time for some unspecified transgression. Though all the Chinese Classics and most educated Chinese rejected, if not the existence of supernatural beings, then at least the existence of the influence of otherworldly powers influencing human lives at a level more *individual* than "fate" or "change," there were and are no fewer credulous folk in China than anywhere else in the world, and Li Po began, from this point on, to glow in the public mind with a truly otherworldly aura. Coincidentally, he also began to appear at the Hanlin Academy, to draft and edit everything from policy documents to ceremonial poetry. And so it came to pass that his work was indeed noticed in the Palace.

The poetry-loving Emperor, like so many of Li Po's upper-class patrons, was apparently also entranced by Li Po's alien looks and his outlandish behavior. (Many sources state that he had the "outlandish appearance" of a denizen of the western region of China, and he was, at the very least, very tall.) Finally, in legend, came a pivotal day. The story goes that Li Po was "sleeping in a Ch'ang-an tavern" (or lying in a drunken stupor), when the call came from the Palace: the Emperor requests the poet's presence, hoping that he will produce a few brand-new poems celebrating the occasion at hand. "We are sorry, Your Majesty, but your humble subject is disabled." Another request, and another lame excuse: and then there came the *Imperial Command*, which received the insouciant response that the God of Wine did not deign to attend the Emperor at present. We can hear the silence surrounding the Emperor. More silence. And then the Emperor laughed. Try to imagine the tension at Court as the (probably apocryphal) messages are sent and refused, and the uproar that broke the expectant stillness to greet that Most High Laughter. Some of the laughter doubtless came from Li Po's enemies: surely *this* witty boy wouldn't last long.

So Li Po lived perhaps a little over a year as a presence in the Capital and as a regular poetic servant at court. The lovely poem with the incredibly long title, "Submitted at the Imperial Command, A Poem Written by the Dragon Pool in the Spring Garden While Viewing the Newly Greening Willows and Listening to the Hundreds of New Songs of the First Nightingales," to be found on page 107 is an example of the sort of poetry he was *asked* to produce. The poetic craftsmanship is superb, and the joy of creation courses through it, I think; but this poem, though it might even be a great poem, is not a "Li Po poem." The creation of poems like this kept him at Court, maybe even in the social circle of the One Man himself, if not within reach of actual political power. It seems likely that he was banished from the Court because of Yang Kuei-fei's complaints to the Emperor about slights found in a few of his Court poems, complaints that expressed the power of Yang Kuei-fei's sexual hold over the aging Emperor. I'm inclined to think that most of Li Po's poems of political protest were created after he'd left Court, when neither the fear of arrest and exile (or worse) nor the absence of hope for further advancement would tend to help enforce self-censorship.

The legend of his final insult to the corrupt Court is a wonderful one, which would probably be best told, and embroidered upon, in a tavern. The story involves an extremely powerful Court eunuch named Kao Li-shih and a pair of street-soiled boots. In any culture where there are harems, there are eunuchs. It's not just the violation of "property" rights that bothers the polygamous "husband," but the "pollution" of the legitimate line of dynastic transmission. Generally speaking, no anatomically correct adult male other than the Emperor himself was ever permitted in the Chinese Imperial harem. That left the Emperor's government in many cases dependent on the word of the Emperor's private secretary, a eunuch of course, for all kinds of orders, including, in some periods after the T'ang, death sentences to be carried out immediately.

Kao Li-shih was a eunuch who took full advantage of his advantages. He was powerfully corrupt, the more so as the Emperor lolled toward senility with the help of his enabling darling, Ms. Yang, the "Precious Concubine." Now, stage right, as if entering the Palace from the street, one eight-foot-tall drunken cowboy-swordsman: assume rain, think mud, mixed with mule dung, and camel dung, and horse dung. Picture the big cowboy splashing in it, boots reaching up above those high knees, then splashing inside, covered with it. If you've never witnessed a pair of tall riding boots being taken off with the aid of servants, you can see what it looks like by treating yourself to the classic film *Tom Jones*, based on Henry Fielding's seminal comic novel of eighteenth-century Britain. The task could be brutal and demeaning, since by the time both boots get pried off, the servant, the human shoehorn, is covered with whatever was on the boots. Drunk indeed Li Po must have been if he had not realized by the time he was done that he had created something new to him: an enemy for life. Now he had a real enemy, and then he was gone from the Academy, the Capital, the Civil Service, banished, never to return, and never again to hold a government job.

Then for twenty years he wandered, writing great poems, but finding fewer and fewer wealthy and powerful patrons.

He was saved in the end from total ignominy. At the close of his life in this world he was nursed through failing health by a real friend, a patron who was simply a good man and who, as an artist, was probably the man best equipped to understand him, in his earthly weakness and crowning glory. At least Li Po died in bed, a mortal man whose body had wasted away. And so we have the story of one last genuine friendship, with a man whose name we do know, Li Yang-ping, the famous calligrapher. According to Waley's biography, Li Yang-ping was born nine years before Li Po, and outlived him by another ten years. He and Wei Hao, another friend to whom Li Po had entrusted an earlier manuscript of his life's work, had the works copied and distributed, after his death, among a trustworthy group. So, though the physical body was wasted, the body about which Li Po always cared more, the body of his poetry, was given the chance to achieve what we love to call Immortality, and the legends to grow toward mythic status.

And though all they could do, for all their love of the old man, was nurse him to a dignified death, by doing so they helped create the final legend, the capping myth, letting the world believe that the blithe spirit Li Po died while drunk of the divine madness engendered by the image of the immortal beauty of the moon reflected in the water, drowned in its embrace.

There are something like 124 poems in this book (including those gathered under a single title). I have divided them into five parts of roughly equal lengths. The divisions are intended to capture aspects of the poet's life and to bring to bear within each section the pretty untrustworthy timetable that scholars have provided for his life. The categories into which I have divided the aspects of his life are drinking, friendship, philosophy and spirituality, protest, and "travel." The fifth category includes poems of travel through the "real world," travel through space and time, and the journey of emotional and intellectual experiences that mature a human who is willing to truly live every day. It also includes a few poems I call "spirit travel," a term I'll define a little later on.

By creating these groupings, I've tried to

make it possible for you to watch the poet grow and change. The fivefold view of Li Po's life that this approach gives us magnifies the scanty help that we get from the known time frame of his life, from biographical scholarship, and from the datable poems. We get five different unfolding views of his life and maturation process. We see him drinking less and less, or less and less frequently. We see his friendships deepening. We see his philosophy move from a simple hedonism toward a rational mix of mature Taoist and even Confucian thought. We also see him begin to address the *Buddhist Tao* (the Chinese say that "the three Ways, or Taos, are One") and to move toward a more and more serious meditation practice, Taoist and Buddhist. We see him move from selfish ambition to an almost Confucian identification with the needs of the common people as he embraces the social duties of the educated man. Finally, we travel China with him at many different times, ending at Fall Cove, a poetic home something like the spiritual home his physical self must have found in the final friendship with Li Yang-ping.

Li Po is the best-known Classical Chinese poet outside China today, and everyone who knows his poems at all knows his drinking poems. It's easy to see him simply as a hedonist, and we should be good judges, living in a hedonistic age as we do, with a deluge waiting in the wings, maybe. But though Li Po surely was a hedonist as a younger man, many of his poems show him using drinking and drunkenness as a means to search for something far beyond even a romantic's vision of "freedom." There is often something almost Dionysian, almost magically freeing, in his poems, even moments that sound like wobbly *satoris*. But (how like a Taoist!) he never uses the Chinese words for *satori*, or sudden enlightenment, to describe any physical, philosophical, or spiritual state he reaches.

Whether it's a case of enlightenment or hangover (and sometimes a drunken stupor is just stupid, for sure), many "drinking poems" could go elsewhere in the book. The poems in part one that open the book are, then, what I'd call drinking poems proper. These range in spirit from riotously joyful through riotously destructive, but there is also a strangely riotous yearning for release that is easy to identify with as the young man's first, maybe almost unconscious, yearning for enlightenment.

At the other end of the scale are the drinking poems written for patrons. These poems are a little less rowdy, and occasionally not just somewhat subdued but, as the relationships cool, even rude. Several of this sort of poem have sprouted like weeds among the poems of friendship, but Li Po can be funny when he's rude, of course.

The poems truly of friendship include some of Li Po's best pieces. The subject lends itself to the display of the best of human feelings. I doubt that it's right to claim that this theme is the most common among the thousand or so poems in Li Po's complete works, but the percentage, carefully calculated, would probably surprise at least all us Westerners. Li Po often lived by making and *keeping* friends. He couldn't be a hypocrite or a fake: the word would get around. Arrogant he was indeed, perhaps hiding a naively loving nature somewhere inside.

In his T'ang China, friendship was a deeply held value, even an honored one. Loyalty was the highest value of the educated male, and friendship was the primary vehicle for learning to express loyalty, as well as the honesty and sincerity on which loyalty must be based. And, of course, friendship is a form of love.

In this second part, there are poems to patrons and to acquaintances as well as poems to his oldest and closest friends. Because it seemed to me when I worked on them that they revealed something about what was required to become a "friend" of the poet, I have also included a couple of directly insulting poems, the other side of the coin of friendship, if you will. One is written in a tone that could be accepted as either insouciant or as just plain insulting. It's written to a Buddhist figure who apparently represented himself as an authority figure. Li Po was always desirous of offending authority, or of appearing to offend or defy authority if, or as much as, he could *get away with it*. The other poem like this is one written to a Confucian, or possibly to a Taoist who has upbraided Li Po for his attacks on Ssu-ma Ch'eng-cheng, the Taoist Master who advised against drinking. Here we see real anger from Li Po, and real arrogance, I think.

There are a few examples among the poems of friendship that have their share of the riotous joy of the young men's drinking songs, but there are many poems of true friendship without a hint of alcohol. If real drinking songs have been allowed in, it's likely because they seemed to me to be truly joyous anthems to good times shared that could not have been achieved other than with real friends. Among these poems there are many, many references to T'ao Ch'ien (365–427), a complex figure and a poet of complex poems. One such complex poem by Li Po, likening himself to this immortal "literary friend," is analyzed, with Chinese text, in the appendix, beginning on page 203. T'ao was known, in the simplifying manner of the legend makers, as a Taoist hedonist and drinker, and it is to these features that Li Po most often points when giving "compliments" to patrons and newly met acquaintances. But he points to more complex levels in T'ao Ch'ien's life and work when talking to or about lifelong friends, and occasionally when treating *himself* to a dose of Li Po–style hyperbolic poetic praise, as you'll see if you delve into the analyses in the appendix. T'ao also appears as a preceptor and a companion on the Way in several of the philosophical and spiritual poems of part three.

Some Western philosophers argue that there is no philosophy in traditional China, but that's just quibbling over terminology; such quibbling Chuang Tzu would doubtless say is what *constitutes* modern Western academic philosophy. As for our poet's intellectual and spiritual concerns, they seem as unsystematic as you'd expect from a poet, but I find Li Po attempting to understand and deal with the problems of "Life" in a direct and serious way.

So, in part three I have drawn together poems that, although they may feature drinking into and beyond oblivion, attempt to address the "true meaning of life," certainly a "philosophical" issue for the traditional Chinese. I

have also added poems that seem to directly re-
cord what we would easily see as spiritual quest.
Some of these poems are very clearly, even lu-
minously spiritual.

If Li Po doesn't, according to the received
wisdom, fall among the Classical poets like Tu
Fu who are embraced today for their alliance
with the downtrodden common people, it may
be because puritans in both China and the West
refuse to read beyond the youthful hedonism of
his early poetry. But even beyond the mandatory
pacifist, anti-war position almost forced upon
him by his identifying *officially* with the Taoist
ideological party, to which the Emperor himself,
conveniently, belonged, it is *easy* to find anti-war
poems created with a brilliantly delicate art that
could not spring from other than feelings deeply
true.

Nonetheless, the selected poems of part four
may appear the most unusual. Though Li Po was
clearly involved in what may have been merely
"Court intrigue" during his brief visit to Ch'ang-an,
legend rooted in facts insists that he was involved
in real confrontations with the more corrupt ele-
ments of Hsuan Tsung's government. At any rate,
he didn't come to the Capital with a desire to "fit
in" and thereby win a sinecure. He got that oppor-
tunity with his practically instant appointment to

the Hanlin, the highest, most celebrated official employment in the realm, outside the uppermost executive levels of the central government. Maybe he believed his talents as a poet could win him entry into that hierarchy, but I doubt that he did. His poetry reveals him as an egotistical man, but few celebrated artists can resist that occupational hazard. The poetry that reveals a powerful ego also reveals a brilliant man; and alcohol aside, a man able to intrigue and manipulate with the worst of them, so to speak. When he faced off with the Emperor, announcing that as the God of Wine he was not subject to earthly commands, he could be *almost* sure that his Emperor would chuckle, and recognize the actual nature of Li Po's relationship with wine.

But it was, without a doubt, a daring play. Li Po was no Meng Hao-jan—great poet, superior man, but subject to stage fright. Angry emperors could put you to death! If we trust the legend, Li Po gambled ego to ego with the Emperor, and daringly came away with a prize, of a sort, but when Yang Kuei-fei quite properly found a couple of poems about beauties whose beauty had distracted kings and emperors into destruction (and some others perhaps even less personally flattering), she was offended, and Li Po was on his way away. Because Yang Kuei-fei was among the several corrupters of the ultimate power, she was powerful, and evil. And to oppose her was courageous, not merely egotistical. If Li Po was a brave man, he was not a fool. The Taoist knows best of all when to withdraw, to retreat, to survive.

Along with the poems written while he was actually at Court, among Li Po's "protest poetry" in part four I would place all of what may have been conventional Taoist-inspired anti-war poems. Li Po's are at least good, full of the horrors of hand-to-hand combat in the desert, powerfully descriptive of wasted landscape and desert space. But you will also find many poems in this section that are less conventional, subtler, and stronger, though they have no blood and no carrion crows gorged on warrior's flesh. Then, as he endures his exile, as he travels for years away from the Court, we find him really discovering the people for whom political protest poems are to be written, the people who will never appear at Court, who will not even begin to appear in large numbers drafted into the Imperial Armies until after the An Lu-shan Rebellion, when Li Po had only a few years to live. These were the people drafted as "cannon fodder" before cannons existed, as ill-armed living shields to draw arrows from barbarians or rebel hordes. They became the subject of protest poems by Tu Fu and others. But Li Po knew them first.

When I discovered Li Po spending the night, and sharing the food, the stewed water weed the locals sarcastically call their "rice," I was surprised. (See "Passing the Night at the Foot of Five-Pines Mountain," page 130.) It's a poem that hasn't been translated until now, so far as I can tell. Here Li Po records his *humbling*: he has nothing to pay for the kindness done him, nothing but to write his poem indicting the government for leaving the honest peasants in such straits. When, at another stop in a lonesome trek, we find him wishing that he could go up the hill the next day with the woodcutter, we know that he is wishing for *honest* labor. It's a real man he wishes to accompany, not just one of the stereotypical "fisherman and woodcutters" who abound in poems of Taoist retreat that begin to appear in conventional poetry later in the T'ang.

The final set of poems, in part five, might be entitled "Traveling in the World," or maybe better, "Finding the Way Home." Li Po spent most of his adult life traveling. Although most of his "popular biography," the legends and myths created by his worshipful readers, takes place at the extreme edge of Chinese civilization in the cowboy country of Kan-su and Ssu-ch'uan, or at the very center, in the dynastic capital at Ch'ang-an (with some time in the secondary capital at Loyang), in fact, very little of his adult life was spent in China's West, and only a little over a year was spent in the Capital before he was exiled from it forever. He was married three times, but during the larger part of his life spent less time with any of his wives than he did in taverns and in the loving arms of professional female "entertainers." Thus we are not surprised to find so many poems about his travels: bragging to all about his trip over the mountain roads that brought him out of Kan-su and down to Ch'eng-tu, the beautiful capital of Ssu-Ch'uan (Four Rivers) Province; and again, understandably, telling us of the flight through the gorges of the mighty, rapid-strewn Yang-tse, in a tiny craft powered only by a small sail and "sculling" oar, and *perhaps* a few more oars and oarsmen—a trip that must have seemed like sharing the stoop of a falcon on its prey, flying bareback down the dangerous headlong dashes down from Ssu-ch'uan, eastward into the center of Chinese civilization.

There are long, boldly imaginative poems in this section, and as you would expect there are also *quatrains*, flashing fragments of things that maybe only a poet's eye, only this great poet, could catch with the eye and in the heart, to be rendered into poems or lines of poems "recollect-

ed in tranquillity," or rounded up from among in-
toxicated dreams. There are poems written to de-
parting friends. Some of these are placed in parts
one or two, on drinking or friendship, but a few
have stayed here in part five, to remind you that
travel was both dangerous and immensely time-
consuming, and that farewells, since each one
might be forever, were exceedingly important.

Finally, in among the poems of "real" travel, I
have included a few poems, long ones like "Over
Heaven's Old Mama's Mountain in a Dream, at a
Farewell Party" (page 148), which may even have
been written under the influence of something
other than alcohol, and shorter ones, like "In
the Old Style: Westward over Lotus Mountain"
(page 155), in which the poet wanders the sky
with a beautiful female spirit but cannot make
himself draw his eyes away from the barbar-
ian warriors below, "Wolves, with men's hats on
their heads." Some Taoists regularly practiced
a kind of "spirit travel" in meditation, and, of
course, Li Po realized that travel in the imagina-
tion, and even "imaginative" re-creation of "real"
travel, were all valid and even necessary pursuits,
or journeys, of any great poet. Realistic descrip-
tion of "real" travel may make a metaphorical
point, or it may simply allow the description,
and communication or sharing, of the beauties

of the natural world. The travel of the spirit, or of the imagination (is the difference a meaningful one?), knows fewer boundaries. You might even say that the little quatrain entitled "Thoughts of a Quiet Night," which is examined in detail with the Chinese characters in the appendix (see page 216), a poem widely regarded as one of the poet's greatest, is also a spirit travel poem, since in it the poet (or his imagination, or his spirit) rides the moon for a visit to his far-off home, or, most painful possibility, fails to be able to....

So here they are, five subjectively, even intuitively, chosen groups of poems. In my mind there are drinking poems that melt away gently into poems of friendship, and those poems into the next part. There are about as many poems that the *translator* thinks of as philosophical or "spiritual" as there are poems of social protest. In the process of searching for a way to present these poems that would show the development of the poet from a wild boy to an ambitious manipulator to a truly mature, thoughtful man, I came to feel that the "Fall Cove Songs" (see "Notes to the Poems" for a physical description of the place they come from) represented, maybe even intentionally, the several stages of his travels: they begin with manifest longing to return to the Capital and end with Li Po's meeting with a strange monk who *is* perhaps a *white cloud*. There is something very close to the actual end to both his physical travels and his spiritual voyage here. After his final stay at Fall Cove, in the Autumn of his life he had another voyage to make, his last voyage, with his friend Li Yang-ping, to help him on his way; but the man who is presented in his final set of poems seems to me finally beyond the desire to travel.

It came to me that these poems represent in a wonderful sense the homecoming that capped Li Po's lifelong quest, at first for fame and even perhaps for power. Here he capped that necessarily vain quest with a realization that his art was his true quest, that the beauty of his creations was, and would remain as long as human beings read, a glory to be shared among all who seek beauty. Maybe it was at Fall Cove where, with a laugh toward old age (when the face in the mirror sprouts white hair a million miles long . . . go look and see), he truly ceased even the wandering of the *white cloud* himself, and fell, into the moon, in the water, at the end of the branch. Not drowned at all, but pulled back into her bosom by the mother we share with him, our Earth.

Part One

Drinking with a Hermit Friend in the Mountains

Together, we drink: two mountain flowers,
  opening.
A cup, a cup, and then, to begin again at the
  beginning, another cup!
I'm drunk, would sleep . . . you'd better go.
Tomorrow, come again, with your lute, if you
  will.

Goodbyes in a Chin-ling Wine Shop

The breeze breathes the shop full of willow
    fragrance,
the prettiest girls in Wu press drink on us,
    forcing us to try . . .
Chin-ling's best have come to see me off.
I want to go, but I cannot go until every toast is
    answered.
Life's ever-eastward-flowing stream . . .
or the loving thought that rides it, which is
    longer?
You tell *me* now. . . .

Bring On the Wine!

Good, fine, truly gentle men, fit to guide the
    people . . .
have you noticed? The Yellow River comes
    pouring down
from the sky, and rushes straight to the ocean,
        never to return. . . .
Good, fine, true gentlemen, haven't you noticed
flecks of white, where once pure black silk
    shined
back from the mirror, even in this sunlit tower.
By sunset there will be purest snow.
Of what there is that may give joy I bid you
    take, and taste.
Don't let this precious barrel rest lonely in the
    moonlight.
What Heaven's given us to use, we *must* make
    use of. . . .
And when a thousand gold are gone, there will
    be more.

So boil the ram, and slaughter the ox: there's joy
    in those,
and if you *can* you *must* down three hundred
    cups at a sitting.

O Grand Master Chin and your disciple T'an-
   chiu, I've offered you your wine, my friends:
   we can't refuse it!
I'll sing you a song if you'll bend an ear:
"The austere music of the ancients, bells and
   drums alone,
is just the warm-up to the feast. Once I've begun
I'll drink me drunk, and never never sober.
From high antiquity on down, the best have
   dwelt unknown;
only us drinkers get our names writ.
Old King Ch'en lived quietly in the Peace and
   Pleasure Palace.
We'd never know his name at all, my friends,
   but for
ten thousand measures of wine, and just enough
   heedless revels."
And if the host cries out, "The wine runs low"?
There's always more where that came from. . . .
I have a five-flower horse, and a *cloak* worth a
   good thousand gold!
Call the boy and send him out for *more good
   wine*!
And we, the three of us, will drown all the grief
   of all the years.

Waiting for Wine That Seemed Like It Never Came

A huge jade jug, the kind they bind and seal
    with fine green thread!
Paid for ... maybe that's why it came so slow.
All my mountain flowers giggled, laughing in
    my face!
Kissing the lip of a wine cup might have made
    them quiet.
The wine did arrive, at last, brought to the
    eastside balcony,
And then, flown back on the breeze from among
those flowers: the most beautiful of Orioles was
    here.
Spring breeze, a lonely drunken man,
and today was perfect.

Hsiang-yang Song

The falling sun will drown before he sees the
    west side of Hsien Hill
Me, my hat on upside down, I'm just lost among
    these flowers,
and all the little ones of Hsiang-yang applaud
    me,
jamming the streets to sing the "White
    Horseshoe" song,
while everyone asks what they're laughing
    about!
They're laughing themselves to death at me,
    their Lord Shan,
good governor, once, though almost always
    drunk as mud . . .
"Bring me my cormorant ladle!
Bring on the fine parrot cup. . . ."
In a hundred years, a lifetime, there are three ten
    thousands plus six thousand days.
Every one of those days I'll drain three hundred
    cups.
Always over that way's the river Han, a pretty
    mallard green,
just the look of good grapes as they start to
    ferment. . . .

If the river ran wine,
we could gaze down on it from a tower freshly
    built of grape skins!
Here's my steed, worth a thousand in gold,
    bring me a young lady!
I'll laugh as I sit in my carven saddle, and sing
    her "Plop Fall the Plums,"
let the poetry classic itself make my case for her,
and hang the wine jug at ready in the carriage as
    we ride away,
with an escort of Phoenix pipes and dragon flutes.
Li Ssu recalled his favorite hounds as he went to
    execution here so long ago.
I won't do that, not me.
Do you see the stone table Hsiang-yang folk
    erected for their good Lord Yang,
carved head fallen away, all covered in moss?
I'll shed no tears, I don't feel sad. . . .
Pure breeze and bright moon, priceless, they
    don't cost a penny.
Hsi K'ang, pure jade mountain of a man, drunk,
even you came crumbling, crashing down. . . .
Give me a Shu-chou ladle, a strong knight's cup:
Li Po will live and die as you did.
King Hsiang had his night of clouds and rain.
    Where is he now?
The River flows east from here.
That sound in the night is gibbons crying.

Post Drunk, Three Little Ones for My
Cousin the Great Official

I

This day, a feast in the bamboo grove.
Our house is blessed with a Great Official!
But after three cups he's little Yuan again,
and once he's really drunk he gushes the purest
    madness....

II

In the skiff in the oar-sound's antique purity,
in the middle of the lake in the heart of the
    moon,
we would be floating home, if the white terns
    would let us,
but they fight to let the wine-soaked, crumb-
    caked
tablecloth fly free.

III

There a clean silhouette of Gentlemen's Hill. It's
    good,
at Ping-p'u where the grand Hsiang's waters
    flow.
At Pa-ling the wine's in infinite supply....

Let us, by drinking, drain the pain from
     Autumn
or, dead drunk, have died trying.

Lines on the Road

Lanling's best wine's heavy as gold with
> turmeric:
In the jade cup it's almost tiger-striped by the
> light.
Any good host here can get me drunk enough
to forget where I am, even to lose the way *home*.

Drunk, Written at Wang Han-yang's Pavilion

I'm like a partridge!
Starting south at the first chill of Autumn,
but lazy when it comes to starting to fly north
    again.
I was timely indeed to follow Han-yang's orders:
I went right off and got some *drink* (or was it
    drunk?).
I'm riding the moon back to his place with it,
maybe a little slow at that, too.

Two Songs for the Autumn Festival

NINTH NINTH AT DRAGON MOUNTAIN
The Ninth, at Dragon Mountain, drinking.
The pretty girls, laughing at me, a "great official,"
drunk, watching his hat fly away on the wind.
The dance, the love, the moon: held me, here.

RECALLING THE NINTH NINTH
Yesterday we *climbed high:* but enough of that.
This day we can raise the goblet up again.
Some find chrysanthemum has a bitter flavor.
Not so much I can't do the Double Yang once
     more.

The Ritual Wailing and Elegy for Hsuang-
ch'eng's Great Brewer, Old Master Chi

Old Master Chi in the Yellow Springs,
better still be brewing your "Old Spring."
The sun never rises on the Night Terrace.
Who do you suppose is there, *already* running
        up my tab? . . .

*Spring, I Come Home to Our Old
Hideaway in the Pines*

I came home to the south side of the southern
　　peak.
Not a thing even a little bit different from the
　　old days . . .
Where I looked, no change in the water in the
　　creek,
nor, where I gaze again, are the rocks
　　　　beneath the rocky cliff even a tiny bit
　　　　different.
Roses, that will be red, now start
　　　　to show green once more beside our
　　　　east window . . .

And the dodder grows around the northern
　　wall again.
How long since we parted, then?
Trees and underbrush are a few feet taller.
For the time being, my fate's in the goblet . . .
pouring alone, or with Mr. T'ao, in the
　　lengthening dusk.

Hsiang-yang Song

I

Where we always played in Hsiang-yang,
singing, dancing to the day's most popular song,
the city wall was moated by the greenest water.
But flowers in the moonlight still led each of us
    astray.

II

"Mountain Lords" we called the apes when we
    got them drunk.
Drunk? They got just plain *nailed* down by
    Gao-yang,
with fancy white headdresses wrapped around
    their heads,
and they'd fall off the horse and then climb
    right back on again.

III

View Peak leans right out over the Han River.
The water's green, the sands beside like snow.
Up on top there's a plaque with an inscription
    that drips tears,
but the green moss has long ago grown away
    the ending. . . .

IV

So get drunk! Splash in your own home pool.
Never even think about the story on the
    plaque. . . .
The Mountain Lords lust to mount their
    stallion, and they don't
give a damn if us Hsiang-yang boys die
    laughing.

Part Two

For Wang Lun

Li Po was on the boat and the boat was about to
      be sailing
when all of a sudden comes the sound:
a great mad troupe, trippingly marching and
      singing:
Peach Blossom Pool is deep,
a thousand *chang*, so they say. . . .
But it's nowhere as deep as the love
you show me, just to see me off so. . . .

Seeing a Friend Off on the Way to Shu

I've read, as you've read, and *I've* seen it myself:
the Tsang-tsung Road is a weird and terrible
    craggy thing,
an unearthly, *unnatural* way to be going.
The mountains rise flat up in your face
and the clouds rise straight out of your horse's
    head.
But then you'll come to the Chin plank road,
with its living canopy of fine-smelling trees,
and soon to all the swelling waters of Spring
as they swirl into the Ch'eng-tu moat.
"Rising" and "Falling"? We all know the saying:
    they're fated!
So get up! Get up, my friend, get on your Way!
There's no need to ask the ancient seer;
wasn't *he*, after all, called "Mr. Flatt"?

Alone, I Pour at Clear Creek River—Rock,
and Write to Send to Ch'uan Chao-yi

Bottle in hand,
I climb out on this great rock.
Since Heaven and Earth began
it's stood a thousand feet above the water.
I raise my cup and smile at the sky,
and the Heavens whirl until the sun shines out
    of the West!
I could sit here on this rock *forever!*
hanging my hook like the wise men of old.
At least I'll send this to those who came before
    me here:
may the music I make, make harmony with
    yours.

Homage to Meng, Greatest of All Teachers

Oh, how I love you, my Illustrious Meng-
    fu-tzu!
You have always displayed the elegance of a
    delicate breeze,
and the whole world knows it!
As a pink-cheeked boy you turned aside the
    offer
of a ride to Ch'ang-an with the prestigious Han
    Ch'ao-tsung. . . .
And now your white head naps with the clouds
    among the pines.
Once, drunk in the moonlight, confused by your
    Classical studies,
or drowned in your cups of sage wine,
you couldn't find your way out from among, or
    under,
the *flowers*, in time to come to the service of our
    Lord. . . .
Now, where on your mountain peak
            am I likely to look up and find you?
I shall begin my discipleship by tracking my
    lord to his lair
purely by his special fragrance, so pure and, well,
    so pure. . . .

Seeing Off Meng Hao-jan at the Yellow Crane Tower

Old friend, I see you off, saying goodbye
to the West at Yellow Crane Tower.
You'll go down through the mist
of late Spring blossoms to Yang-chou,
your lonely sail a distant shadow
in the green emptiness, until all that's
left to be seen's the Great River itself,
flowing beyond the sovereign borders
of the Kingdom of the Sky.

*Seeing Off My Friend Ho, Going South
Again*

Mirror lakes, flowing streams, rippling clear
    waves.
With this mad traveler's returning boat, there
    will be high spirits.
Mountains' shadows and *this* man of the Tao: it
    seems as if
        they've met before.
What can I say: you're trading the Imperial
    Yellow Earth of the North
        for some southern barnyard, silly old
        goose.

*A Joke at the Expense of My Dear Friend
Cheng Li-yang*

T'ao Ch'ien, the famous official, was drunk,
    drunk every day.
Never even knew when it was Spring at the hut
    he called Five Willows.
The sound of his lute, purity itself, because he
    never let the lute be strung.
He unwound his official headpiece to filter
    muddy wine of its lumps of yeast:
and when the job was done, he wound it back
    around his head to dry,
napping in the pure breeze, under the north
    window.
He called himself a servant of Fu-hsi, lord
    before all lords of men.
When these days would you find his like: firm
    and reverent? Deep inside a chestnut?
At a single glance anyone can see! You'd be close
    as brothers all your lives long.

Jeering at Wang Li-yang

The whole earth is white, the wind the very *color*
        cold is:
the flowers of snow that fall through the air are
        as big as my hand.
T'ao Ch'ien would die laughing
if you refused the "thing in the cup," as he so
        delicately called his *wine*.
Do you find fondling a lute a lewd thing?
Do you think to cultivate "five willows" in
        retirement,
as this master did, is a vain or a foolish thing?
Do you wear that fancy official head wrap of
        yours,
all unaware that its true purpose is to strain the
        rough stuff
                from good murky country wine?
You and I ... what do we have in common?

Answering the Master of the Buddhist Association of Hu-chou, Who Has Enquired about "this Po Fellow"

I, Gentleman-in-Retirement now called Green
    Lotus, am,
in fact, a Taoist Immortal banished from
    Heaven.
Under this present name I have happily hidden
in taverns and bars for thirty springs.
But since the Master of Hu-chou's Buddhists,
    himself,
for some reason desires to know who I am:
I am the reincarnation of the Buddha of the
    Golden Grain,
and thus, also of Vimalakirti, who never spoke a
    wrong word.

Seeing Off Fan, the Mountain Man, Returning to Mount T'ai

Lu's travelers go to embrace Longevity's
    Crane. . . .
You leave me to make your way to Mount T'ai,
first, on your way like a slip of cloud,
dark, mysterious, there amidst the blue cliffs,
high, high up, clear to the Gates of the Heavens.
You can gaze on the sun, so close you could
pull it to you, or climb on.
Clouds and mountains, you cannot gaze
    beyond.
From such a glorious parting as *this* one, when
    could you return?

*By the Riverside, Seeing Off the Lady
Master of the Tao, Who Travels with
the Three Precious Gifts to the Southern
Sacred Peaks*

Wu River, Lady Master of the Tao:
in her turban she wears a lotus.
Her rainbow robe is charm against all the rains
    of the Yang-t'ai.
Well traveled are the shoes, the soles beneath
    her feet:
with each chaste step she purifies the earth.
She seeks a mountain of a Taoist man
    somewhere up on the peaks,
and she will see him there, her husband, Mr.
    Wei.

Banquet with Cheng Ts'an-ch'ing at His Mountain Pool

You fear the grass is late to green this year.
I shudder that the ruddy faces certainly are
    fewer
and I'm sad to see the willow flowers fly. . . .
The wine we've bought is perfect, the one right
    thing for this.
The sound of song to send off the setting sun. . . .
Shadows of the dancers whirling round the
    crystal pool!
The day is dying and we haven't drained our
    cups. . . .
With whom, who's the perfect one, or two,
to share what's left of our happiness?

Down Chung-nan Mountain and Overnight, with Wine, at Hu-ssu's House

When the sun fell through the trees, I headed
        down
the mountain, moon behind me all the way.
Gazing again to find the path I'd come,
I found, finally, only a chill darkness. . . .
But you met me just there,
and led me home to your little farmstead.
The youngsters rushed out to open the gate,
the green bamboo, one more dark path,
with creepers brushing, catching at our clothes.
Then, your happy welcome in, and my heart at
        ease,
good wine poured back and forth,
and song in harmony with the pine wind.
Song done, we found few stars left
        in their river in the sky.
I was *drunk*, and you were happy too.
Happy the two of us, all thought
        of the world's ways forgotten.

Three, Five, Seven Word

Autumn, breeze, pure-and-clear.
Autumn, moon, bright-as-day.

Fallen leaves gather, and scatter again.
Cold crows perch, and start and settle again.

We think of one another, all the time:
       for us to meet is hard. . . .
In this season, on this night, feeling at all
       is a difficult thing.

Seeing a Friend Off, Returning to Wu,
over Wine, Thinking of Ho Chih-chang

There was a madman in Ssu-ming,
free as the breeze, as the wind blowing: Ho
    Chih-chang.
Our first face-to-face on a Ch'ang-an street,
and he bruited me about the "Exiled Immortal."
He did dearly love what T'ao Ch'ien called "the
    thing in the cup,"
but he's transformed now: just dust beneath the
    graveyard pines.

Parting at Thorngate

Passing far beyond the Thorngate Narrows,
we've come wandering out of Ch'u.
The mountains and the cultivated plains will
    both end now
as the Great River flows on through the
    wilderness.
The moon rises like a flying mirror,
and the clouds grow into towers out above the
    sea. . . .
Yet it's the waters of *home* that will carry you on
    now . . .
and only my thoughts will ride on with you now,
    a thousand *li*.

Overnight with a Friend

To bathe, to let float away the griefs of a
    thousand ages,
and then to drown
in a hundred jugs of wine.
A pretty night, perfect for talk, for *philosophy*
and a moon so bright. What sort of man could
    sleep?
Finally, finally *really* drunk, we slept
in the open, on the mountainside,
Heaven and Earth, our covers, our pillows.

Drifting with Our Friend the Governor on Magpie Mountain Lake

I

At first you think you're close to Magpie
    Mountain,
but then you realize there's a lot of lake between
    you and the peak. . . .
Well, our little trip is really just to help make
    parting bearable,
so the oars dip to a leisurely beat as we return.

II

This lake's some ten miles wide,
yet the mountain's green shines shimmering all
    the way across.
On the western sky the slender crescent's just
    slipped from the veil of dusk-light,
as we set the last of our departing friends
    ashore.

III

The water here runs into North Lake.
Our craft's coming back from the southern cove.
Looking back as we turn, *it* seems to turn too:
as if the Magpie himself were coming to see me off!

Thinking of East Mountain

I

Long time since I turned toward East
    Mountain.
How many times have those roses bloomed?
All the white clouds of those days scattered.
Whose house is it that the bright moon shines
    on now?

II

Today I came hand in hand with a little Miss
    Hsieh,
Sighing long for all those friends no longer able . . .
Hear me, all travelers East Mountain bound!
We've opened the pass, and swept the white
    clouds clear.

On Hearing That Wang Ch'ang-ling Has Been Demoted and Exiled to Dragon Point, I Wrote This and Sent It on Its Long Way There

Yang Chou's flowers are all fallen, the "Come
    Home" birds all call:
I've heard Dragon Point's beyond all five of the
    Five Streams.
I send you my Autumn-heavy heart and the
    bright moon.
May they follow the wind straight on even there
    to the west
        of where the Ye-lang's barbarian
            kingdom once stood.

*From under the City Wall at Sandhill, a
Letter to Tu Fu*

I've come here, why? What shall I say?
But though the walls of Sandpile City
aren't the scholar's classic lofty perching place,
there are a few good ancient trees where
    Autumn's insects
perch in the sunset to sing as always of time
    passing. . . .
True, you can't get drunk on the wine of Lu,
and Ch'i's songs are empty of that feeling of
    beginning again
        that can raise a hero's heart.
Yet, thinking of *you*, I've risen
to write, even if it be upon the running water,
to send to you across the watery vastness
to where you campaign in the South.

A Poem, from Grain of Rice Mountain, for Tu Fu

Here, on top of a grain of rice (or of a mountain
    so named),
I've run into you, Tu Fu, again!
And you in a hat as big as a plate, big enough to
    keep off the whole noonday sun.
All I can say is it looks like you're losing weight.
Is poetry so bitter, so bitter, my friend?

Presented to Officer Lu

With these Autumn colors all around,
           there is no far or near.
Step out the door and you *are* on Cold
      Mountain,
and white clouds can recognize each other
           from a long way off,
as you knew me, and then waited for me among
      the cold
               catalpa trees.
Well, I have a question for *you*, old friend:
           That oldest of old black cranes of
               yours?
When it flies west, how many years
           till it comes back home again?

In Repayment for an Invitation from Mr. Ts'ui

That bird-track grass, the delicate style
of the calligraphy you wrote
inviting me to come out drinking at Lute Creek ...
the track of *your* hand over the pure
perfect white of the little scroll like a brocade
of cloud stretched across the Heavens.
Done reading it one more time,
I try to smile into the enclosing emptiness,
seeing you sitting facing me again.
Then I sing your words one more time,
words, tracks, traces seeming proof against
the ravages of these days of fire and sword,
safe here in the sleeve of my robe,
completely untouched, these three years.

For Ts'ui Ch'iu-pu

I

I love Ts'ui Ch'iu-pu,
he's a breath of the air of the kind and obliging
                Magistrate of Peng-tse.
He's planted five willows in front of his gate.
There are two *wu-t'ung* trees planted by his well.
Mountain birds drop in to listen to the sessions
          of *your* Prefectural Courts.
Flowers drop from the eaves into your wine.
I can't let go of you, I cannot bear to go.
My heart-and-mind go round and round
               endlessly, without a plan.

II

Judge Ts'ui's studied T'ao Ch'ien, when he too
    was stuck judging.
He's found a north window, where he can paint,
               or nap away a summer
                  morning
He carries his lute, and even lets the moon play
    on it.
His heart, too, hears a music he can play
    without the strings.

When he entertains a guest, he keeps on
        pouring

                        till the jug is on its side. . . .
When he serves as an official, it's not for love of
        money.
Your eastern acres look ready for Spring
        plowing.
If you *really* want it all in wine grain, you'd
        better plant it pretty soon!
and write your "Coming Home" even earlier
        than he did. . . .

III

As flowers are to Ho-yang County,
jade is to Ch'iu-pu, the man.
A place will follow a good man's name,
                and better itself,
as the air of a place, a good wind indeed,
                kindles from its heart
the glorious transformation that is Spring!
Its waters come in timely fashion
straight from the River of Stars,
bringing even the bare mountainside
the look of a new-painted screen.
Think gratefully now of a traveler straight
from the Emperor's Gates of Gold
and cast a handful of sand in condolence
for Ch'u Yuan, poor lost Minister of Ch'u.

For a Lady I Met on the Avenue

This powerful horse steps proud, tramping the
    fallen blossoms.
Nonchalantly, I tapped my crop, brushing
    against her Five-Cloud Carriage.
The beauty gave me a single smile from behind
    her pearl-screened window,
then pointed toward the faraway red mansions:

"There I dwell," she said.

Part Three

Question and Answer in the Mountains

Ask me how it is I've come to perch in these
    blue-green hills,
and I'll smile with *no answer*; I'm happiest with
    heart-and-mind just so, may be. . . .
Peach blossoms float by here, gone into the
    quite *definite* shadows.
There is another world, other than this one we
    choose to live in.

In the Old Style: A Pretty Face

A pretty face will last no longer than a lightning
    flash,
a season's glories ride a wind away.
The grass was green, frost's white.
As sun falls west, east, moon's on the rise.
The fullest, blackest tresses thin and fall,
and with the tiniest puff of breeze are withered
    weeds.

There were saints and sages in the ages past …
    of each of all, who mastered *this?* Master Pao-p'u
saw the bones of the proud and virtuous
    transformed
into bones of apes, or yet, the more to mock our
    dream
of immortality, into the bones of cranes.
And mean and greedy folk? See there those
    worms and
bugs, struggling in the sand?

None here's even a match
for Chuang Tzu's fool Kuang Ch'eng-tzu,
madly bragging himself on a cloud, or a wild swan,
just flown away.

In the Old Style: Chuang Tzu's Dream

Chuang Tzu's dream's a butterfly,
a butterfly effortless at work at being Chuang
    Tzu. . . .
For the one body, the Whole Thing, there is
    nothing
                 easier than change.
Everything's good, even peaceful, when it's
            viewed from far enough away.
So we see, and so we should know it: waters
    from beyond the
deepest seas of myth rise and flow again from
    mountains:
            clear, shallow, running rivulets.

Once upon a time a man sold melons at
    Greengate,
who had, sometime before, been bowed before,
            as Lord of Shao.
Wealth and power, even these go so . . .
Oh, let us fortify our place, put a guard here,
build up a strong point there . . .
            for what?

A Farewell Banquet for My Uncle, the Revisor Yun, at the Pavilion of Hsieh T'iao

It's broken faith and gone, has yesterday: I
    couldn't keep it.
Tormenting me, my heart, today, so full of
    sorrow.
High wind sees off the Autumn's geese, ten
    thousand *li*.
Facing this, it's fitting that we drink here.
We write as if from P'eng-lai, or from the days
    of Chien-an.
And fittingly, Hsieh T'iao is clearly heard here
    once again.
All embracing, his thoughts fly free,
mount to blue heaven, to caress the bright
    moon.

I grasp my sword and strike the water, still the
    water flows.
Raise the cup to drown your grief, grief only
    grows.
Life in this world: few satisfactions.
In the dawn light, hair unbound, I would drift
    free in the skiff.

Song for the Road

The Great P'eng flew, so sad, and it shook all
    eight directions!
In the middle of the sky it broke down, so sad,
    strength used up.
Just the leftover wind from its flapping, so sad,
    has made
        the storms of ten thousand
          generations.
If you can make it to Fu-sang, so sad, you might
    find it
        hanging there like a robe of stone:

People who've gotten there since then? They've
    passed on the tale.
But when Confucius died? So sad, who of all his
    sniveling disciples
even dropped a tear?

I Banish Me

Face to face with the wine:
eyes shut, or shutting, unconscious
of darkness,

while the falling petals filled the bowl,
the lap of my gown . . .

Still drunk, I got up, to walk on the moon
in the water. . . .

The birds had all gone to nest;
humans, also, had grown few.

In Imitation of the Ancients

The living? You pass them on the road.
The dead? They're home already.
From Heaven to Earth, the briefest trip,
the same sad dust to dust, ten thousand ages.
The rabbit in the moon stays
at work at his mortar and pestle,
but the *Fu-sang* tree's already turned to kindling.
Dry bones sleep: they have nothing to say
when graveyard pines green to Spring's coming.
What we call *glory* floats on air. . . .
How could that be the prize?

Autumn on My Heart, on My Mind

Spring's Yang, I *remember*. Warm? Spring was
    hot
                as yesterday's sudden sun.
I remember, in a blue tree, singing, Yellow
    Oriole.
Jungle grew like a raging fire,
fresh with *fragrant* orchids that sank in the grass
                as every sunset does.
Then you stand in a breeze and it's a cold wind
    blowing.
The sky is full of the smoke of the farmers'
    stubble burning off.
Trees' leaves all fall. Moon freezes.
Even the sedge worms can tell it's not *right*.
Even in meditation all my heart and mind can
    find is Autumn:
every fragrance, flocks of flowers like herds with
    their rams . . .
all gone at once. White dew: frost, the cycle
    frozen, finally.
Nothing's final. Mud, darkness. Beginning again

Drinking Alone under the Moon

I

Among the flowers, a jug of wine,
drinking alone, with no companion,
I raise my cup to invite bright moon,
And then, with my shadow, we are three.
The moon doesn't know a thing about drinking.
My shadow just follows me around.
Yet I'll go with moon and shadow,
joyfully, until the end of Spring.
I sing and the moon dances,
I dance, and my shadow tumbles.
Sober, we share the joy we knew.
Drunk, each goes his way.
Forever bound to ramble free,
we'll meet again, in the River of Clouds.

II

If Heaven didn't love wine,
there wouldn't be a Wine Star in the Heavens.
If Earth didn't love wine,
there surely wouldn't be a town named Wine
    Springs here on Earth.
Heaven and Earth both love wine, therefore!

There's no way loving wine could be an offense to
        Heaven.
I've heard clear wine referred to as "the
        enlightened."
Moreover, all call the murky "the wise."
Both the original sages and wise men were
        drinkers . . .
Who needs to search for precedents among
        spirit Immortals?
Three cups and you'll *know* the Great Tao,
a single dipperful and you'll be one with *nature*
        naturing. . . .
Just get to what goes on within the wine,
and you'll know what no sober man
has ever learned
(or at least been able to pass on).

III
Pretty little birds sing on the sweet breeze . . .
falling petals embroider the air.
Who can bear a Spring alone?
Success! or Failure. Cranes' long legs; ducks',
        short?
Creation and Change could not create or change
a one of them. They are ordained before. . . .
All the things of this world are, and have
always been, therefore, hard to pass judgment
        upon.

Ah, but after you're drunk you can't hit the sky
(or the ground) with the arrow of *blame*.
Steadfast as any headless man, you'll sleep
    alone.
To not know I have a me, myself . . .
this is the deepest joy.

IV

Deep melancholy may have a million causes:
the cure's a mere three hundred cups of wine.
Sorrows *are* without limit, and, for sure, there's
    a limit to wine,
yet empty one pot and all sorrow's gone!
It is just because of this *mystery* that we name
    our wine *the Sage*!
A wine-sweetened heart opens wide to all
    nature. . . .
Po Yi, Shu Chi, *Good Men*, resigning even grain,
    starved at Shou-yang,
While Yen Hui, most precious student of
    Confucius,
"often empty," as the books brag, suffered
    hunger, and died young.
In those bygone days they didn't enjoy drinking.
Their *fame* is what was empty. What's the use?
Crab claws in the river Hsiang turned even gold
    to gravel,
and Ch'u Yuan's golden reputation into sand.

The Taoists' fabled P'eng-lai Island's
                    just a giant heap of brewer's leavings.
You can drink good wine,
and ride the moon, drunk, over the tallest tower.

*Looking in the Mirror and Writing What
My Heart Finds There*

Get the Tao and it's permanent Paradise,
Lose it, and what's permanent is change,
or withering, or old age, if you need it clearer. . . .
So I laugh at the man in the mirror,
with that hair like dead weeds under frost,
and get back a sigh from that big all-knowing
      eye.
And from that door my heart knocked on, I ask
me, how did I get so like a withered tree?
T'ao Ch'ien and Me, peaches and plums,
sweet juicy fruits once: Old man,
let's hope when our strings run out
we'll at least get buried properly,
on the warm side of your South Mountain,
with someone singing that song from the *Poetry
Classic*, about how we're all immortal.

Again, It Weighs Heavily upon My Heart

Thinking it over and over again, in one final
        quatrain . . .
I grasp, gasping, to go east, where the River
        goes.
To raise the cup there one more time! But with
        whom?
What's Mount Chi without my dear old Ho?
Memory of desire: the oars stop, the barge full
                of wine and girls turns, about to go
                        back.

I Looked All Over the Mountain for the Monk, but Not Finding Him, I Wrote This

Path of stones goes up beside Cinnabar Creek,
pines like a gate, shut, and moss and lichen in
    the shade,
with bird tracks on the closed-in stairs.
No one there to open the meditation hall,
so I peek in the window and see a white prayer
    whisk
hanging on the wall, growing the "dust of the
    world."
It draws a vain sigh from me.
I *want* to be gone, yet I *want* to stay, *round and
    round.* . . .
Fragrant clouds, everywhere, rising from the
    mountain,
and a rain of flowers from the sky.
There's already an emptiness full of music and
    goodness.
How much the more so when I hear
                the pure wail of the gibbons.
It's clear I should cut free of the business of
    being in the world.
In this place, in this way? Can I know?

T'ung Kuan Mountain: A Drunken Quatrain

I love the music of T'ung Kuan Mountain.
I could stay a thousand years here, never leave.
I'd just keep on waving my dancing sleeves,
till I've swept clean the Mountain of the Five-
    Trunked Pine.

Visiting the Tao Master of Tai-t'ien
Mountain When He Wasn't There

You can hear dogs barking in the sound of the
    water here,
and peach blossoms sparkle from the rain.
Where the trees are really deep you'll see a deer.
No one's here by the stream, but I can't hear the
    temple bell.
Wild bamboo slices through the sky's bright
    white-clouded blues,
and the cascade tries to fly free of the jade-blue
    peak.
Nobody knows where you've gone.
A sadness like Autumn: I lean on a pine here, a
    pine there.

Sitting at Reverence Mountain

The flocks have flown high up and gone.
A single cloud fades into emptiness.
In meditation endlessly we two:
then only the Mountain of Reverence.

Thoughts of a Quiet Night

Before the bed, bright moon light.
I took it for frost on the ground.
I raised my head to think of the moon,
then bowed my head to dream of home.

Part Four

Submitted at the Imperial Command,
A Poem Written by the Dragon Pool in
the Spring Garden While Viewing the
Newly Greening Willows and Listening
to the Hundreds of New Songs of the First
Nightingales

The East Wind is already greening the grass of
    Ying-chou.
In the purple palace with its red towers we come
    to see
                and feel the fertility of Spring.
South of the pool the color of the willows is full
    halfway to Spring green,
and delicate tendrils of mist wreathe the palace
    wall,
       while hundred-foot threads of willow
hang down from the carven pillars.
Above, the obedient birds sing together in
    harmony:
within these grounds they find the Spring
    comes early.
Spring breeze goes reaching up through blue
    clouds, and out,
to a thousand gates and ten thousand doors
    where all hear Spring's music!

For today, as with the Ancients, "the King is in
	Hao-ching,"
and five clouds of color hang brightness,
leading, a-sparkle, up toward purple purity. . . .
And he goes forth from his Golden Palace,
following the sun through the seasons,
returning from Heaven in his jade cart,
he goes for a turn among his flowers,
starting at P'eng-lai to see the dance of the
	Immortal Cranes,
and turning homeward through the Yi-shih
	Garden,

where the first nightingales were heard to sing.
And those first nightingales flew, circling up, in
	the Grove Garden,
Begging to enter the mouth-organ sound of
	their song
among the voices of the concert of the
	Emperor's phoenix flutes.

A Spring Night in Loyang, Hearing a Flute

From whose house does the jade flute's song
                come flying into darkness,
spreading on the Spring breeze, *filling* Loyang?
All hear the sound of branches breaking, the
     mark of parting . . .
and whose heart does not fill with thoughts of
     other gardens, other times?

A Song of Bathing

If it's perfumed, don't brush your cap;
if it's fragrant of orchid, don't shake your gown.
The world hates a thing too pure.
Those who know will hide their light.
At Ts'ang-lang dwells a fisherman:
"You and I, let us go home together."

In the Old Style: Moon's Tint

Moon's tint can't be swept away;
the traveler's grief, there's no way to say it.
White dew proclaims on Autumn robes;
fireflies flit above the grasses.
Sun and moon are in the end extinguished;
Heaven and Earth, the same, will rot away.
Cricket cries in the green pine tree;
he'll never see this tree grow old.
Potions of long life can only fool the vulgar;
the blind find all discernment hard.
You'll never live to be a thousand;
much anguish leads to early death.
Drink deep, and dwell within the cup.
Conceal yourself, your only treasure.

In the Old Style: I Climb High

I climb high, to gaze upon the sea,
Heaven and Earth, so vast, so vast.
Frost clothes all things in Autumn.
Winds waft the broad wastes cold.
Glory, splendor: an eastward-flowing stream,
this world's affairs, its waves.
White sun covered, its dying rays,
the floating clouds, no resting place.
In lofty *wu-t'ung* trees nest lowly finches.
Down among the thorny brush the Phoenix
    perches.
All that's left, to go home again.
Hand on my sword I sing "The Going's Hard."

Moon over the Pass

Bright moon suddenly *up* from beyond Heaven
    Mountain,
where it had lain hid in the dark, endless sea of
    clouds.
The long winds came down tens of thousands
    of miles,
from the north to blow through Jade Gate Pass.
Here Han troops climbed the road to Paideng
    Mountain,
because the barbarians wanted our Great Dark
    Sea in the desert.
Of all who stood upon that ancient field,
I've never heard one returned.
Armed sojourners, they gazed hopelessly
homeward over barren ground,
their hearts gone home: read the bitter faces.
In home's many mansions, facing *this* same
    moon:
        the wives and loved ones also
sigh and see clear, in the mind's eye, yet can't let go.

War South of the Wall

Last year, war:
at the Sang-gan's source.
This year, war:
        along the Tsung-ho Road
Our whole army washed weapons in the
        Tiao-chih Sea,
and set horse to graze on the grass that grew in
        patches
underneath the snows of the T'ian Shan Range.
Three thousand miles of battles,
three armies exhausted, withering away, *grown
        old. . . .*
The Huns farm these battlefields for bones:
since the time of the Ancients, nothing to see
but bleached bones on yellow sands, their fields.
Ch'in built the Wall to keep them out.
Han fed the beacon fires to burn unceasing,
yet the War went on:
war, wasteland: men dying there.
The horses of the conquered neighing skyward,
        mourning.
Vultures feed on man guts.
With flesh in their beaks they fly up,

fly up to hang those guts in the withered
    branches.
Soldiers die, blood splashes brush and grass.
    Generals?
Is all this done in vain? You know that soldiers
are the direst of instruments. The wise make use
    of them
only when there is no other way.

A Song of Farewell at Red Cliff

Two great dragons, hands on the same sword,
already at war, deciding who's to be cock and
    who hen.
Red Cliff's towering ships, brushing the Sky,
    tethered to Earth.
Bows drawn flat, arrows aflame, sky flat aflame:
clouds ablaze, and water reflecting the flame.
Chou Yu won his fame here, came the Cock,
where he broke Lord Ts'ao, to Hen.
Gentlemen, go look upon the Great River,
gaze out over the roiling blue.
 An Emperor Whale and his little lady flopped
    up abruptly here once,
and they left these walloping wallows for us to
    see!
Now one after another the books will flow,
    recording what the Ancients saw here!
And I, a pure young man, will henceforward wish
that I should carry a swordsman's soul within me.

A Soldier's Ballad

Big black mane bay horse: it's almost a boast
just to sit astride this white-accoutered stallion.
Booty of war!
In the sand where the moon is the color of cold,
here: an iron thunder from the drums up on the
    city walls.

War South of the Wall

Battlefield: darkness: confusion, is it fog?
Men at war, or ants all swarming . . .
air's heavy; sun, a bloody red chariot wheel:
blood drying purple on bramble.
Crows argue the ends of man guts like reins.
They eat at the gate of our grief, and them so
    full,
they can't fly free of it.
Yesterday: men on the walls;
today: ghosts who cry beneath it.
Great banners of bloodlust,
gauze spattered with crimson
droplets like tiny stars.
The pulse of the war drums throbs,
throbbing, endless.
This wife's family: husband, sons . . .
the blood of the pulsing of the drums.

Jade Stairs Lament

Jade steps grow white dew.
Night, late, has its way with her silken hose.
So let the crystal curtain fall. . . .
In its jingling glitter, gaze on many Autumn
    moons.

The King of Wu's Favorite, Just a Little Drunk

The breeze moves the lotus blossoms,
the River Palace all perfume.
The King of Wu is feasting in the Gu-su Tower.
Hsi-shih's delicately drunken dance
beguiles with its perfect weakness:
all-inviting, perfect Yin.
Smiling, leaning by the white jade
cool bed, by the East Window,
where the Yang will rise.

Tzu Ye: Ballads of Four Seasons

SPRING

Lady Luo Fu, of the land of Ch'in,
plucks mulberry leaves by the green water side,
delicate pure white hand over the deep green
    leaves,
makeup brighter red in the clear fresh light of
    the sun.
"My silkworms aren't hungry, I must go.
Oh, Lord of Five Horses, stop not here, don't
    stop here at all."

SUMMER

Mirror Lake's three hundred *li* around;
lotus blossoms blooming: toward midsummer,
when beneath the fifth moon Hsi-shih plucks
    them,
the people watch in a crushing crowd.
She turns her boat back without waiting for the
    moon . . .
going home to her love, the King of Yueh . . .
home to her lover, King of Yueh.

AUTUMN

Above, Chang-an, the City of Long Peace,
from ten thousand mansions the lonely clash,
the clash of clubs, is only the "fulling,"
the preparation of the long-stored Winter robes
for Winter use again. The Autumn wind
is not done blowing yet.

WINTER

He leaves tomorrow, the messenger has told her.
So she sews her warrior's cloak all night,
but the needle's cold as a warrior's
steel to her delicate fingers.
How can she bear to touch the scissors *blade?*
Now she's done: she sets it on its perilous way,
and starts to count the days till it might reach
    him. . . .

Song for Seng Ka

The True Monk's Dharma name is Seng Ka.
From time to time he has instructed me in the
    Three Carts.
I ask a word and he intones a mantra
that contains just a few thousand universes as
    they pass,
the words of his mouth, and the miracles of
    Kuan-yin returned,
words in rivers of sands and sands in rivers of
    words.

This monk first lived in the southern bamboo
    sky of India;
Dharma's Law brought him here to live as a
    recluse in our land,
a man beyond all moral error, beneath our
    eternal sun,
brightening our Autumn moon.
Heart-and-mind, upon our world, a greening
    lotus.
In thought: the cleanest, purest.
In appearance: a roof beam hewn square from a
    log of the purest frost.

Nothing there could be in any way diminished,
nor, to what is there, could anything be added.
"In his bag," the people sing, "there is a Buddha's
    bone a thousand years of age,
and in his hand, the Monkey's staff, ten
    thousand!"
Alas, I know his earthly soul has wandered the
    rivers and lakes since I was a boy.
It was an event both rare and strange that the
    True Monk spoke to me of being and
nonbeing, and in a single word, wandered all
    through the Brahmans' land,
once more bringing order to all who are
    confused,
and doing away with all frivolous transgressions
    and invasions of filth.

A Pa Girl's Song

The river Pa goes like an arrow;
Pa boats just seem to fly.
In the tenth month, if he left *then* . . .
what time next year may he be back again?

Two Ballads of Ch'ang-kan

I

My hair barely covered my forehead then.
My play was plucking flowers by the gate.
You would come on your bamboo horse,
riding circles round my bench, and pitching
    green plums.
Growing up together here, in Ch'ang-kan:
two little ones; no thought of what would come.
At fourteen I became your wife,
blushing and timid, unable to smile,
bowing my head, face to dark wall.
You called a thousand times, without one answer.
At fifteen I made up my face,
and swore that our dust and ashes should be one,
to keep faith like "the Man at the Pillar."
How could I have known I'd climb the Watch
    Tower?
For when I was sixteen you journeyed far,
to Chu-t'ang Gorge, by Yan-yu Rocks.
In the fifth month, there is no way through.
There the apes call, mournful, to the Heavens.

By the gate, the footprints that you left:

——

each one grows green with moss,
so deep I cannot sweep them.
The falling leaves say the Autumn's wind is
    early,
October's butterflies already come,
in pairs to fly above the western garden's grass.
Wounding the heart of the wife who waits,
Sitting in sadness, bright face growing old.
Sooner or later you'll come down from San-pa.
Send me a letter, let me know.
I'll come out to welcome you, no matter how far,
all the way to Long Wind Sands.

II
All I, your wife, with all my heart recall
before you, is the innocence of a maiden's
    sequestration.

And then, I married my Ch'ang-kan man.
Now a woman, I stride the shore and read the
    clouds
to learn whence come the winds and where's my
    man *now*.

In the fifth month of the lunar year,
the south winds rise, and my heart's with you,
coming down through Pa-ling.

——

In the eighth month the west winds rise:
I know you're departing Yang-tzu.

You come and you go:
what would I be if my heart weren't torn? . . .
Our meetings are few. We live apart so long.
But you'll be here from Hsiang-t'an soon,
and my dreams have carried me over the wind-
    driven waves. . . .

Then, last night, a wild gale passed through this
    place.
It blew down riverside trees. Water, water, dark
water in a limitless darkness, and where were
    you?

If only I could ride those scudding clouds,
to find . . . to know . . .
ending in the final joy of finding you,
somewhere east of Orchid Shore.

Mandarin duck and drake, their beauty,
lifelong mates, they swim so beautifully
    together.
And the kingfishers too; they will never fly
    apart.

———

Would I lament marriage at only fifteen,
my face by nature bare with the beauty of peach
    blossom,
to become the lifelong wife of a river merchant?
My eyes are bright, tearing as I gaze into the
    Autumn winds.

Passing the Night at the Foot of Five-Pines
Mountain in the House of the Widow Ao

I spent the night at the foot of Five-Pines
    Mountain,
silent, solitary place; at first
there seemed no welcome there.
This Autumn's hard for the villagers;
I hear a neighbor woman in the cold
pounding the last grains from the husks,
as we kneel to eat the water weed my hostess
    calls "our rice":
moon's glorious light from the empty white
    bowl.
And I'm ashamed I can never repay
this kindness, gentle mother.
Three deep bows will never make a meal.

Part Five

Overnight at Shrimp Lake

Cockcrow I set off down Yellow Mountain;
by dusk I was plopped in Shrimp Lake for the
     night.
White rain, or sleet, or hail? I was blinded in
     sunlight
on that cold mountainside, the silver
bamboo a forest, a forest of lances,
and then, almost frozen, gray-faced, thrown
     down
thrown down, like a babe on their doorstep.
You folded a lotus leaf for a basin
and carefully bathed me. . . .
At midnight, the High Heavens opened:
the River of Stars blazed in our eyes.
This morning I go on to a great mansion,
down to bow, and scrape.
This just to let you know
I'd rather be with you, old axe-man,
there, across the great gorge
cutting, among the trees, among the clouds.

The Road to Shu's a Hard Road

The Road to Shu's a hard road.
Ow! Aaaiii, be damned!
Talk high? Say murderous!
The Shu road's *hard*.
Try climbing the sky!

They say the Lords Ts'an Ts'ung and Yu Fu
founded a kingdom here; but it took
forty-eight thousand years to build the way
     through
to get here from there, from settlement to
     settlement,
up and over the border passes to get a thing
     "built,"
anything in a place like *here*.

And west of here, there's the Great White
     Mountain . . .
there the road's *for birds only*
toward the peaks of Omei.
The mythic five, the great muscled warriors,
     died in sudden landslides
building the stairs of stone and the wooden ladders
that hooked it all together.

At the very top, six dragons guard the sun;
down in the gorges, back-swimming waves
seem to try to stall the river's getting on.
Yellow cranes can't fly across;
gibbons and monkeys, aspiring to rise,
sulk at their valley-mired fates.

Green Mud Mountain? It coils and winds.
Getting through the boulders at the glacier's
    base: nine turns to every hundred steps!
Touch the constellation "The Triad," pass by the
    Well Stars, too,
gazing in awe, and clutching your chest,
even sitting down you'll be gasping for breath.

When will the traveler, heading west, turn back?
These cliffs are just too dangerous to climb.
Birds cry mournfully in ancient trees,
males pursued by females flutter through the
    forest,
listening to that cuckoo, crying to the moon,
voicing her sorrow at the empty mountain.

The road to Shu is hard,
harder than climbing the sky.

Bold men's faces pale on just hearing of these
    perils!

Clustered peaks, barely a foot from the sky,
withered pine trees, upside-down, hanging over
cliffs,
flying waterfalls cascade with deafening din.
Boulders roll and thunder into ravines far below.
With danger like this, after traveling so far,
I wonder why I wanted to come up here at all?

Sword Tower stands on one of the steepest
spots;
if one man guards this path, ten thousand won't
break through.
But what if bandit wolves and jackals hold the
paths?
In daylight we may face down tigers,
but at night we must avoid the gnashing teeth
of blood-sucking serpents, or end up lifeless,
dead empty sacks.

The dream of Ch'eng-tu, the Brocade City,
shines before me,
but is it as good as just going home?

The road to Shu is hard,
harder than climbing the sky,
but I'll crawl on westward with a heavy sigh.

Omei Mountain Moon

Omei's Harvest Moon is on the wane,
but half's enough to fill the P'ing-ch'ang River.
Into this darkness I leave Clear Creek for the
    Three Gorges,
Heart-and-mind filled with him whom I can no
    longer see,
as we move downstream of Chung-ch'ing.

Down to Chiang-ling

Morning, from White Emperor City,
among the many-colored clouds . . .
and then, a thousand *li* in a single day, to
Chiang-ling.
From both banks, the apes' cries, unceasing.
This little boat: gone beyond ten thousand
mountain ranges.

Climbing the Five Old Peaks of Mount Lu

South and east of Lu Shan: *the Five Old Peaks.*
Sky's blue's pierced by the points of these golden
    hibiscus buds.
Here among the Nine Great Rivers you can
    reach up and tie together
                every color of the blooming
                 earth.
Here, someday, I'll build my nest, among the
    clouds, among the pines.

Gazing at Heaven's Gate Mountain

Heaven's Gate Mountain's cleft opens to let
    Ch'u's river through.
Blue-green, running east, reaching here it turns.
On both banks green peaks stand, facing.
My sail rises with the new day's sun, beside it.

Egret

The white bird settles on the Autumn waters,
flies alone, settles like a snowflake.
Heart, mind, set, ready: *won't go yet*.
We stand alone beside the sandy islet.

In the Old Style: The Yellow River

The Yellow River moves eastward into perfect
    darkness.
The white sun falls in some westward sea.
Even the river marches away, flowing full of
    time's light,
every thing a flutter on a sudden breeze, even
    love lost.
Spring's face is the face of a youth, and that's left
    me too.
And where Autumn first shows his face,
        the more withering changes have
            begun.
No man's a pine; in the cold we simply die.
No one's stayed young long.
But I can wish that I could ride
a dragon of cloud so young his horns were yet
    to grow.
I'd snort up *everywhere* and hold the reins that
    hold the light.

After the Ancients

I walk into the river
        to play in the clear Autumn stream.
I love them, lotus blossoms so fresh.
Pluck lotus, tip it, play with the pearls
until there's nothing round left in the roiled
    water.
My beauty,
        you're lost in the multicolored clouds
I so desire to give you that gift hidden
        by the distance to the Heavens:
Though we think of each other, there is no way
        (even on tiptoes) to see.
I stand so long my heart grows taller, drawn out
    of me,
gazing into that cold breeze, toward you.

A Song of White Clouds: Farewell to a Friend

The mountains of Ch'u and of Ch'in—in both,
       there's no lack of white clouds.
They will always follow and find a true
    gentleman. . . .
You go now into the mountains of Ch'u.
The white clouds will follow as you cross the
    Hsiang River,
and there, across Ch'u Yuan's great river,
you will find a gown of the moss called *lady
    tresses*.
Sleep there, and when you rise, rise early, and go
    home.

Gazing on Lushan Falls

Sun reflecting from Censer Peak purples the
    clouds
to the look of incense smoke.
Gazing deep, it's the skein of the water I see
    bursting forward,
hanging where the stream goes: flying, flowing
    into froth,
then plunging straight down, three thousand
    feet, like the River of Stars
come falling down from the Ninth Heaven.

In the Old Style: I Got to the Islet beneath
Wu-shan

I got to the islet beneath Wu-shan, the
    Mountain of the Shamaness,
searching the Ancients' way to "climb the Yang
    Tower."
But the *Heavens* were *empty*, the multicolored
    clouds destroyed
as if by a war at the walls, by water, by fire and
    sword. . . .
And from the far-off *earth* only the clear wind
    came. . . .
The *spirit-of-the-female*, gone *from this place*
    already a great long time,
And King Hsiang, where could he be?
What had been, in fact, wild dissipation, in the
    end
                came round to nothing.
Kindling gatherers, shepherds, wander here. Do
    they weep, do they wail?

Climbing the Peak of Great White

Up the west side to the peak of Great White
    Mountain,
as the sun set I was exhausted from the straight-
    up climb,
when Great White spoke to me:
"Open the Heavenly Gate for me.
I want to ride the cold wind away . . .
straight out, where the clouds float."
I could raise my hand and almost touch the
    moon,
and make my way forward, as if there were
        no mountains there at all.
Once we've parted, when I reach Battle Hill,
will we ever meet again?

Over Heaven's Old Mama's Mountain in a Dream, at a Farewell Party

Sea travelers talk about *The Island You Lose
    Your Voice About,* but
mist and waves hide it. It's hard to tell how
    much you can believe. . . .
And Yueh folk will tell you all about Heaven's
    Old Mama's Mountain:
but there the clouds sometimes deepen, or thin
    to brightness,
so it's always hard to know what you can see.
Heaven's Old Mama goes right on up to Heaven,
              and runs on, on Heaven's edge.
There she towers over the Five Holy Peaks and
    shadows
            the Red Wall Range,
just where the T'ien-t'ai Range's Ridge, forty-
    eight thousand feet high, *already*
begins its turn toward the Southeast.

I wish I could follow them into the Southeast,
in a single night cross Mirror Lake on the moon.
The lake would be lighted by my reflection,
and it would see me off across the Gorge of the
    Yen!

Is the place still here where the great Duke
  Hsieh Ling-yun
    dwelt in seclusion?
The green water in broad clear ripples where the
  monkeys call?
I'd put on his famous cleated climbing boots,
and make my way up the blue cloud stairs.
Halfway up I'd stop and stand in awe at the sun
  on the sea,
and in the midst of emptiness hear Heaven's
  Cock crow.
Confused by all the flowers, I'd lean on stone,
and suddenly, all would all be darkness.
Bears roaring, dragons chant, cascades crash!
The stirring waters give birth to living mist.
Lightning flashes, thunder rumbles,
hills and mountains crumble and collapse.
The Caves of the Heavens, their gates of
  stone,
thundering, crash open upon a blue-green dark
so vast there is no way to see . . .
   all the way down.
Sun and moon sparkle there, a tower of silver
  and gold.
The Lord of the Clouds crumbles to powder
    and comes down in flakes.
Tigers drum their zithers, phoenixes drive their
  carts round

and round and round. The once-men who are
    now Immortal
mountain *hsien* stand in rows like a field of
    hemp.
Suddenly both the *hun* and *p'o* souls within me
    shudder and dance.
My heart ablaze, I awaken, and sigh and sigh
    again. . . .
Only consciousness, now, and pillow, and mat . . .
lost, the clouds and mists of a moment ago.
In this world, when you seek such pleasures,
    isn't the end always just so?
From the Ancients on down, all things go, all
    waters flow on East.
"Goodbye, my friend, my beloved. When will
    we meet again?"

I shall guard a white deer beside a blue cliff. . . .
I shall ride it only when I go to call
                upon the most famous of
                  mountains.
Why would I twist my fair features and bend
    my straight spine
just to greet and do the bidding
                of those in power or those with
                wealth?
Shall I rob myself of this clear face and open
    heart?

Overnight with the Master of Clear Creek House

That night when I reached Clear Creek
      where I'd hoped to spend the night,
the master was still out among the stony cliffs.
From the pillar beneath the eaves hung the
    dipper of stars. . . .
From my pillow and mat, I could hear the
    sound of wind and water.
When the moon fell west of the mountains,
F-f-fah, f-f-fawel, the ape of evening cried.
                I swear it was trying to cry *Fall*. . . .

Summit Temple

This night, in Summit Temple,
I raise my hand and touch the stars.
I wouldn't dare to raise my voice,
for fear I'd wake them, up in Heaven.

Ballad of the Voyager

Sea voyager, on Heaven's winds,
in his ship, far wandering.
Like a bird, among the clouds,
gone, he'll leave no trace.

Climbing Hsin-ping Tower

Thinking of leaving my own place, I climb this
    tower,
and already I'm longing to come home,
    wounded by the Autumn sunset.
The sky seems to have grown, the fallen sun is
    far away.
The waters are pure where cold waves ride the
    flowing stream,
and foreign clouds rise above mountainous
    trees.
Barbarian geese fly above islands of sand. . . .
Dark, a *vast* darkness: how many tens of
    thousands of miles?
To the limit of the eyes' view, everything orders
    me to sorrow.

In the Old Style: Westward over Lotus Mountain

Westward over Lotus Mountain
afar, far off: Bright Star!
Hibiscus blooms in her white hand;
with airy step she climbs Great Purity.
Rainbow robes, trailing a broad sash,
floating she brushes the heavenly stairs,
and invites me to mount the Cloud Terrace,
there to salute the immortal Wei Shu-ch'ing.
Ravished, mad, I go with her,
upon a swan to reach the Purple Vault.
There I looked down, on Loyang's waters:
A vast sea of barbarian soldiers marching,
fresh blood spattered on the grasses of the
      wilds.
Wolves, with men's hats on their heads.

Clear Stream, Midnight, I Hear the Flute

It's a Ch'iang flute, the long kind, and it draws
    the notes
        of "Plum Petals" as far as they can be
          drawn.
At Wu Creek, by the built-up bank, clear water,
    pure feelings.
        I'm reminded that *Ch'iang* flutes can
          converse with dragons.
At Cold Mountain, at Fall Cove, it was the
    moon that hurt the most.
Here, what tears at the guts? Memories of the
    palace, in this sound.

Fall Cove Songs

I
Fall Cove's as long as Autumn itself:
its sighing breath makes Autumn fall on every
     heart,
and a wanderer's heart, already burdened,
may be all the more likely to fall here.
So it's up the eastern tower for the likes of me,
for a long gaze straight back toward Ch'ang-an,
or, straight down, to find the river's water run
     away.
And I'll send *these words* with the river's waters:
"Does your whole heart rest here
with the same thoughts as mine?"
If I row the first clumsy strokes of the way
with my hands full of tears, Fall River will carry
     me
all the way home.

II
At Fall Cove it's the gibbons make the nights so
     sad. . . .
At Yellow Mountain it was my own white hair
     that I endured.
The water's clear, but it's no garden pool,

rather a rushing, roiling, gut-wrenching stream . . .
a place to love to leave, but hard to get around to
    leaving,
and what was to be a little trip's become a
    tiresome trek.
In just what year, I wonder, will I find myself a
    day for my return?
Tears raining into the orphaned boat.

III

Fall Cove's a rare brocaded bird . . .
no place like it in the world of men, and few in
    Heaven.
The famous Mountain Pheasant's put to shame
                by these greenest waters . . .
wouldn't dare let its feathered gown
                be reflected here!

IV

I was a bristle of whiskers when I came to Fall
    Cove,
then one morning I woke up withered.
Turns out the cry of gibbons turns hair white,
till long or short, it's gone to silky wisps.

V

So many white gibbons at Fall Cove,
leaping and swinging up, like snow flying.

They lead their little ones out to the ends of the
    branches,
to drink and to *play*, in the *moon*, in the *water*.

VI

Grief at heart's what makes the Fall Cove
    wanderer
look *close* at Fall Cove's flowers. . . .
Hills and streams like Yen-hsien County,
on a windy day it could be Chang-hsia.

VII

Drunk, I try to climb aboard the mount of the
    Mountain Lord!
Cold, I sing of Ning Chi's cow. . . .
In vain, I chant the poem of the white stone's
    ripening . . .
till my tears soak the black sable robe.

VIII

Of all Fall Cove's double thousand mountains:
the Water Wheel Range is the strangest.
The sky turned over like you tip a cup to show
    it's dry,
until you find yourself expecting gravel to fall
    out . . .
all the tipped-out water comes, strange,
with a rush, over the mistletoe on the branches. . . .

IX

The River Spirit Ancestor's a rock face,
against the bluest sky, swept clear for a painted
    screen.
Poems have been written here forever.
Green characters appear to be brocade
where moss and lichen grow.

X

A thousand thousand stone-cedar trees:
ten thousand myriad pure *girl-child privet*
    groves:
mountains, mountains, white egrets full:
pools, clear pools like open doorways,
where the white apes chant their poems.
Gentlemen, don't come to Fall Cove. . . .
The ape's cry shatters your heart:
it will be the end of your travels.

XI

The soldiers of the watch march straight across
    the bird track.
The River Spirit Ancestor thrusts up behind a
    fishing weir.
The water's fast, the traveler's skiff's an arrow.
But the mountain flowers brush his face with
    fragrance.

XII

The water's like a fresh-spread roll of raw silk:
this place, here, flat as the sky.
Be patient, and you'll ride the bright moon:
watch the flowers board the wine barge.

XIII

In emerald water, a pure white hand, the moon.
Moon bright, white egret, flying.
The boys hear the girls who've been out picking
    water chestnuts.
There's only one road: it rings with their
singing, all the way home.

XIV

Fire of the smelters' furnaces lights up sky, and
    earth,
sparks, red stars, a chaos in the purpled smoke,
making the young smelterers appear to blush
even on a brightly moonlit night.
Their songs move into every curve of the cold river.

XV

White hair! Three thousand cubits long . . .
and a sadness, a sorrow as long.
I do not know, into my bright mirror, here,
whence it's come, this Autumn frost. . . .

XVI

At Fall Cove in a hut with a little field, a good
      old farmer
catches fish that live in the water there.
His wife sets snares for the silver pheasant:
she ties her nets in the brightest sunlight
just at the edge of the deep bamboo.

XVII

A wave laps at the foot of the ancestral hall.
Clearly, it's the sound of words I hear, but there's
      nothing I understand.
In the dark I say farewell to the mountain monk,
bowing politely to the white cloud.

Notes to the Poems

DRINKING WITH A HERMIT FRIEND IN THE
MOUNTAINS (PAGE 37)

When you first read this poem in the Chinese, one
of the things that jumps out at you is the second
line. In the characters, it's "one cup, one cup, *again*,
one cup." What dullness, or what daring? "A horse,
a horse, my kingdom for a horse." Only a Li Po, or
a Shakespeare, can ply that kind of repetition with
mastery. The poet ups the ante in the line, too: the
"again" could very easily be interpreted as referring
to hexagram 24 of the *I Ching*, "Beginning Again,"
which actually appears in this punning manner in
many of Li Po's poems. (See, e.g., "From under the
City Wall at Sandhill," and "Autumn on My Heart,
on My Mind.") If we read it that way, we have our
drunken mountain flowers, *so drunk* that when they
have another cup they think they are starting over,
from scratch, at the beginning. Li Po really raises
the stakes, as a poet, putting his whole reputation
as a poet into the pot with the next line. It's a *direct
quote*, with only one of the seven characters slightly

changed, from the official biography of T'ao Ch'ien, in the *Sung Shu*, the history of the Liu Sung dynasty (420–477 c.e.). This supposedly drunken song contains not only a very fine imitation of drunken babbling but, in addition, an arcane scholarly allusion as well. Imagine the delight of the reader, contemporary of the poet, *or of this translator* thirteen or so centuries after the fact, who recognizes the voice of T'ao Ch'ien in the poem. My thanks go, with a deep bow, to A. R. Davis for his brilliant scholarly work on T'ao Ch'ien, without which *I'd* surely have missed Li Po's dastardly trick. What a wonderful, and fearless, sense of humor this poet had.

Waiting for Wine That Seemed Like It Never Came (page 41)

Line 7, "Orioles": This proud, colorful bird always stands for the highest class of courtesan, a professional female entertainer. She was a beautiful, always literate woman trained in the art of conversation. She was most likely also a master of one or more party games, including playful poetry writing, with the "loser" condemned to down a cup of wine, and even several kinds of Chinese chess, including Go, the challenging chess game exported to the West under the Japanese reading of its name. She was far more than *merely* a partner for sophisticated sexual play.

Surely there are many more meaningful elements in this wonderful mosaic of words than we can identify today. If, as seems likely, this poem was written when Li Po was in exile, only just reprieved from a death sentence, the drunken hedonism might be a functional part of his public persona (that is, he wants to appear to have become a helpless drunk, no threat to anyone), but in this poem Li Po seems to be attempting to associate himself with the tradition of "signifying behavior," of wild behavior in mockery of the Court. This sort of behavior was first and always most clearly associated with the so-called Seven Sages of the Bamboo Grove (3rd cent. C.E.), a group of political outcasts that included the great poets Juan Chi and Hsi K'ang as well as the perhaps purely legendary "drunkard" Liu Ling. T'ao Ch'ien, who followed this group by just over a century, is often seen as a hedonistic Taoist drinker, or just maybe as something closer to an epicurean farmer and family man. In the first guise he was the favorite poet of every one of the T'ang and Sung dynasty greats. In the complete works of Li Po we see poem after poem loaded with allusions to T'ao Ch'ien, the drinker who mocks authority and convention.

As is the case with many of Li Po's longer poems, the grammar and rhetoric of this piece, so different from any we know in the West, may be difficult to find engaging. The poem often lacks grammatical connectives, and depends on the juxtaposition of images and the associations that arise from its allusive material to bring its sometimes apparently disparate sections together into a cohesive whole. This is the sort of thing that two of Ezra Pound's most important "teachers," Ernest Fenellosa and Achilles Fang, saw in Chinese, and from them Pound came to understand, or maybe to create, what he called the "ideographic method."

In this poem, at any rate, Li Po presents himself first as the roistering hedonist we know so well in the West as the God of Wine. We could as easily recognize him here as playing the role of "jester" in Western literature; he speaks truth to power, or at least claims a political motive behind his apparently wild behavior. One of his models, Hsi K'ang, pretended to madness to avoid political persecution but was executed nonetheless, winning posthumous moral fame. King Hsiang's hedonism didn't win him immortality.

DRUNK, WRITTEN AT WANG HAN-YANG'S PAVILION (PAGE 47)

There is a joke in the choice of the messenger bird. The partridge is famous from the earliest references for its quick departure for the South at the first sign of the season's change. The word Li Po uses for "timely" also means "in season." The verb the poet uses for acquiring the wine (which is doubtless what he was ordered or asked to go out for) does suggest (to me at least) that the word "drunk" is meant punningly to be read as a noun, as in "he sent me out to get some drunk and I got some drunk, just for him."

Two Songs for the Autumn Festival
(page 48)

These two songs both refer to the Ninth Ninth Festival, an autumn fertility ritual, agelessly ancient, but perhaps recognizable to us as a variant of Oktoberfest in some aspects of its practice. Nine is the number associated with Yang, and a good bit of the randy humor the two quatrains have in common rests on the association between greater aspects of Yang (for instance, the sun), and lesser, as in all things male. Chrysanthemum enters the poem owing to the fact that it blooms latest in the Autumn. Taken as an infusion in alcohol or tea, it is believed to strengthen sexual vigor and lengthen life. Li Po would also recall its mention in a famous poem by T'ao Ch'ien about, what else, drinking in Autumn.

Spring, I Come Home to Our Old Hideaway in the Pines (page 50)

Mr. T'ao is T'ao Ch'ien, several centuries dead but immortal in his poetry. The poem is most likely written for Li Po's final wife, whom he left along with his two surviving children, but whom he wrote to and about often thereafter.

Seeing a Friend Off on the Way to Shu (page 56)

The Rising and Falling are the traditional metaphors for worldly success or failure: our poet just makes them gravitational. "Mr. Flatt" is a historical or at least a legendary figure, but his name would probably be read as "peaceful" rather than "flat" outside the suggestive context of this poem. Li Po uses all sorts of tricks to help an anonymous friend overcome his fear of heights, and therefore of the difficult road into Shu (modern Ssu-ch'uan). In the poet's "The Road to Shu's a Hard Road" (page 134), where he's bragging about his own conquest of mountains, the difficulties are described as much more daunting.

The puns (on "Way" and "Flatt") that close the poem are very clear in the original.

Alone, I Pour at Clear Creek River–Rock,
and Write to Send to Ch'uan Chao-yi
(page 57)

One of the wise men alluded to is apparently Yen
Tzu-ling, a childhood friend of the later Han dynas-
ty's founding emperor Kuang-wu Ti, who refused
office under the new leader, ostensibly because he,
like this poem's version of Li Po, enjoyed "jus' fishin'"
more.

Homage to Meng, Greatest of All
Teachers (page 58)

Nobody but Confucius himself may be called by
the honorific *fu-tzu*, so the first line is the key: the
poem is an outrageous piece of warfare by poetic
insult worthy of Cyrano de Bergerac. The first
friendly insult is to remind Meng Hao-jan (689–
740 C.E.) of a youthful indiscretion that robbed
him of early patronage, and thus probably of the of-
ficial career that, at least in his early years, he so de-
sired. Then Li alludes rather gently, given the story,
to the time when the handsome and talented young
Mr. Meng, visiting the capital, ended up hiding un-
der the bed of a famous courtesan who had invited
him to visit, not knowing that (in one version of
the story) the Emperor was planning one of his

famous incognito (or supposedly incognito) visits to the "entertainment quarter," with a visit to Meng's lady of the evening as one of the items on his evening's agenda. Dragged out at last shamefaced and mortally afraid from where he had hidden under her bed, he was greeted graciously by the debonair Emperor, and asked to recite one of his poems . . . but, as Li Po's poem tells us, all did not go well from that possibly great opportunity. Meng was "weak to his occasion," to borrow a phrase from the late great American poet Robert Creeley. Suffering stage fright, Meng stammered out a poem that contained a line intended as an expression of humility, but which the Emperor chose to take as an insult, and Meng was sent home into exile.

Seeing Off My Friend Ho, Going South Again (page 60)

Ho Chih-chang *may* be the subject of this poem. He is not known to have traveled south in retirement. Maybe Li Po talked him out of it.

A Joke at the Expense of My Dear Friend Cheng Li-yang (page 61)

Mr. Cheng, probably one of the many hosts and patrons who sheltered and enjoyed Li Po during his travels and exiles, would have understood all the standard references to T'ao Ch'ien. Despite, or in many cases *because* of, the common image of T'ao as a drunken "Taoist," everyone who was personally mocked in a good-humored poem by Li Po could count on having his name (if not his biography) immortalized. The poem itself contains almost every stock reference to T'ao, except a reference to his Utopian poem "Peach Blossom Spring." In line 8, Li Po may have been aiming at a single one of the several possible meanings of the character *li* (basic meaning, "chestnut"), and may have known something appropriate or appropriately funny that his audience would immediately respond to: I've just tried a scattershot approach, using "firm" and "reverent" as well as the basic meaning, "chestnut."

Jeering at Wang Li-yang (page 62)

The reference to the head wrap (a word translated elsewhere as "turban" or "headdress") is an allusion to T'ao's very ostentatiously using his "hat," a badge of rank, in just such a manner. A poem titled with a "jeering" or a "jesting" or the like, like the one above, is often pretty rough even when it is truly purely in fun. This one sounds to me a little more outside the boundaries of good-natured bad taste.

Answering the Master of the Buddhist Association of Hu-chou, Who Has Enquired about "this Po Fellow" (page 63)

The "Master of the Buddhist Association of Hu-chou" has in the original a title that is a transcription of a Sanskrit honorific term that may, when taken literally, refer to a "Buddha" somehow slightly less honorable than the Buddha Li Po lays claim to. In the original this poem is just twenty-eight characters, with an additional twelve in the ridiculously long title. Li Po is certainly playing with the "Master," and the insouciant or maybe even sassy suggestiveness of many of the words has seemed to me to beg for the loose treatment I've given it. The tone of the poem is made absolutely clear by Li Po's identification with the Buddha of the Golden Grain. This figure is the perfect patron of drunks in China, since all "wine" in China is fermented from grains rather than from grapes or other fruits as in the West. Through layers of reincarnation the Buddha of the Golden Grain is also related to Vimalakirti as well as to Li Po himself. Vimalakirti is a favorite of lay followers of Zen: he is famous for not speaking, in a metaphysical argument when *no words* was the right answer. I think that Li Po is trying to take the sting out of his message here. It is sacrilegious, of course, but it is also *silly*.

BY THE RIVERSIDE, SEEING OFF THE LADY MASTER OF THE TAO, WHO TRAVELS WITH THE THREE PRECIOUS GIFTS TO THE SOUTHERN SACRED PEAKS (PAGE 65)

Images such as the Yang-t'ai, Wu-shan (Mountain of the Shamaness), and clouds-and-rain all refer to sexual practice. The Taoist wife and husband were both masters, since gender doesn't intrude upon mastery. Chaste sex (*not* sexual abstinence, but sex practiced within recognized boundaries, for instance, monogamous sex) is well-practiced sex. Li Po is jealous and admiring, I'd say.

THREE, FIVE, SEVEN WORD (PAGE 68)

The title simply refers to the very unusual form, one couplet of three-word lines, one of five, and one of seven. Numbers and number groups are used in many kinds of divination, including the famous *I Ching*, one of the Confucian Classics that was adopted by Taoists and street fortune-tellers. Without any arcane meanings, it remains a pretty poem.

On Hearing That Wang Ch'ang-ling Has Been Demoted and Exiled to Dragon Point, I Wrote This and Sent It on Its Long Way There (page 74)

Li Po has loaded the poem with ancient phrases and place names. I have a suspicion that he has done so to try to lighten his friend Wang's sense of being wronged by providing him with a list of historical "friends" who have preceded him in such a fate. Never more than a minor official, and always regarded as both a great poet and an exemplar of the good Confucian's care for the people under his governing hand, Wang was exiled for a short time after the loss of power of his patron the poet-official Chang Chiu-ling in 738 C.E. Wang had worse luck to come; he was in the Capital again in time for the An Lu-shan Rebellion, during which he was killed in 756 C.E.

From under the City Wall at Sandhill, a Letter to Tu Fu (page 75)

This poem is full of bitterness at the worsening political situation in the mid-T'ang. The original contains a reference to a line from one of T'ao Ch'ien's "Drinking Wine" poems. It also contains, in the reference to the wine of Lu and the songs of Ch'i, an ironic twist on a couplet by the poet

Yu Hsin (531–581), a favorite of both Li Po and Tu Fu.

Lu was the home of Confucius. To say that its wine is weak is to suggest a similar problem with Confucianism. This is hardly a shocking idea to most Westerners, who have generally turned toward the "East" for mystical or "transcendent" thought, but in China, even in the T'ang, when Zen as we know it was born, to poke fun at Confucius, unless you were Chuang Tzu, was edging toward dangerous. Tu Fu was and is known as a Confucianist, but even he supported T'ien-t'ai Buddhism and certain strains of Taoist thought in his later years, when this epistolary poem was probably written.

PRESENTED TO OFFICER LU (PAGE 77)

There is a joke going on here: one of the possible meanings for Mr. Lu's name character, *lu*, is "black."

IN REPAYMENT FOR AN INVITATION FROM MR. TS'UI (PAGE 78)

One of Li Po's very best poems. It leads us nicely into the next three, which make up a veritable catalog of T'ao Ch'ien references as well as giving us an insight into the powerful value that Li Po placed upon loyalty and friendship.

For Ts'ui Ch'iu-pu (page 79)

I–III. If we can trust the pagination of the original text for any help with the dates, Li Po's infatuation with T'ao Ch'ien was a lifelong one. Many Chinese poets, including Tu Fu and Wang Wei of the T'ang, and Su Tung-p'o, the one Sung poet to challenge the prowess of these "big three" of the T'ang, felt the same way. T'ao Ch'ien was, simply, the first "modern poet" worth reading. It would seem he was also a man worthy of emulation in every way. If *I* do another book of translations, it will certainly be entitled *T'ao Ch'ien: Li Po's Favorite Poet*. Ts'ui Ch'iu-pu was also among the three or four people of his own generation who became among Li Po's lasting friends. The next two poems continue the praise of Mr. Ts'ui.

I, line 5: The *wu-t'ung* tree is valuable for oil and shade. Here the word is perhaps used because it's clearly a visual pun. The two characters of the word *wu t'ung* may be read to say, "I'm the same"— that is, "I'm the same as T'ao Ch'ien."

III. When's the last time you saw a mathematical expression in a Chinese poem? In a poem, period? It is a pure ratio: C is to D, as A is to B . . . I haven't been able to carry it any farther, but that may just be because I'm flabbergasted. Almost as strange, for a poem by Li Po, is the casting of praise

176

for Ts'ui Ch'iu-pu in terms with recognizable Confucian sources. Ts'ui had proven himself an excellent official, as well as a best friend, and Li Po was for once able to congratulate a friend without making a joke of it. It's certainly a more mature poem, and perhaps therefore a poem written later in life, than most in this book.

QUESTION AND ANSWER IN THE MOUNTAINS (PAGE 85)

Maybe one of Li Po's most "serious" poems. The seriousness is achieved through a definite playfulness of language. The "question and answer" is *wen-ta* in Chinese, the *mondo* teaching/learning technique of Japanese Zen. In China it was live ad-lib interaction when it began. It is, I understand, less spontaneous in most uses today.

The peach blossoms are a reference to T'ao Ch'ien's Utopia.

IN THE OLD STYLE: A PRETTY FACE (PAGE 86)

The final four lines are, in the original, a patchwork of direct quotes and references, both direct and arcane, to two famous Taoist works, the great *Chuang Tzu* and a far less substantial work, the *Pao-p'u Tzu*, by the fourth-century alchemist Ko Hung, whose works contributed to the rise of popular Taoism. The reference to the transformation of men, great and mean, into apes and cranes (the latter symbols of immortality in both Taoist literature and popular religion) and bugs and worms, may have been read by some in Li Po's eighth-century audience as straight "reincarnations." The magician Kuang Ch'eng-tzu is a sanctimonious fool presented in chapter 11 of the *Chuang Tzu* as the only "spiritual master" arrogant or deceitful enough to suggest that his "Way" could overcome death. The wild swan *might* exist for poet and reader as only the most oblique sort of reference to the very next passage in chapter 11 of the *Chuang Tzu*. I love the original. This is the best I've been able to do at leaving an indication of why that is. Please see chapter 11, "Staying Home, Possessing Nothing," in *The Essential Chuang Tzu* (Boston: Shambhala Publications, 1999) for the whole story on Kuang Ch'eng-tzu and the swan called "Big Goose Dummy."

A FAREWELL BANQUET FOR MY UNCLE, THE REVISOR YUN, AT THE PAVILION OF HSIEH T'IAO (PAGE 88)

The Chien-an period (196–219 C.E.) at the close of the second Han dynasty marks perhaps the first great period of flourishing of "modern" Chinese literature. Hsieh T'iao (464–499 C.E.), a poet-official from an illustrious family of poet-officials, was probably best known for his landscape poetry.

SONG FOR THE ROAD (PAGE 89)

The Great P'eng is a huge mythical bird created by Li Po's favorite philosopher, Chuang Tzu. Chuang Tzu plays with the ideas of differing *relative* capabilities, idealism (moral and ethical), and even flight itself, in the opening chapter of his eponymous book. The word *p'eng* used to name the bird is related both visually and in pronunciation to another word *p'eng*, which, with the meaning "intimate friend," is an essential word in the opening sentences of the *Lun Yu*, or *Analects of Confucius*, the founding text of Confucianism. Li Po uses the same pun elsewhere, and so the last line is not such a surprise to the Chinese reader as it might be to "us English-speakers." The "so sad" repeated in all lines but line 5 is, in the *original*, a deliberate archaism, a formal feature of the Sao and Song styles of the poetry of the Southern State of Ch'u (most famously in Ch'u Yuan's "Encountering Sorrow"). No doubt Li Po includes it here for the mockingly ironic effect it has achieved by the last line.

I BANISH ME (PAGE 90)

Probably written while he was in actual banishment, this is a poem about decision making, and timeliness. It also seems to me a very possible seed of the legend that Li Po died while drunk, attempting to embrace the image of the moon in the water.

In Imitation of the Ancients (page 91)

The rabbit in the moon—the Asian counterpart of the Western "man in the moon"—is seen as pounding a mortar, always busy making the *elixir of life*. The *Fu-sang,* a tree in this version of Chinese moon myths, is associated with a leading character in *another* myth related to everlasting life.

Autumn on My Heart, on My Mind (page 92)

In autumn in traditional China it was the practice of farmers from prehistoric times (before written history) to make the final act of cultivation for the year the *burning* of the stubble of the last crop harvested in any field, returning its ash to the field as fertilizer, while also doing away with any insect pests that might otherwise have overwintered there. The *character* for "Autumn" was constructed (clearly mimicking this agricultural practice) by placing a pictograph of a cut plant next to one for fire. At the next level, by association with various negative things (the hardship of the winter to come, the fact that beloved elderly ones and tender children often pass away in greater numbers owing to the vicissitudes of the season, etc.), one of the words for sadness is constructed by placing the character for "Autumn" over the element meaning "heart."

DRINKING ALONE UNDER THE MOON (PAGE 93)

II: In this poem, Li Po is, perhaps totally seriously, ruminating on what we'd call the *process* of fermentation. Something—*natura naturans*, "nature naturing" or "nature doing what it does"—is going on in the bottle or the jug, that actually produces a substance that appears, at least at times, to bring us closer to "enlightenment." For a student of *alchemy* this would certainly have been a potentially serious question, and we can't underestimate the seriousness of it as a question for the poet. The poem is also, as it appears, a humorous response to the anti-alcohol "party" among official Taoists.

III: Allusions to Chuang Tzu, and to T'ao Ch'ien, begin on line 5 of poem III. The last two lines of this translation are an allusion to T'ao Ch'ien's "Drinking Wine: Twenty Verses," poem V. If I could treat them as I have the two poems in the appendix you would see the nature of the borrowing, but since I can't, please trust me, and enjoy the fact that there is an art present here beneath the level I can show, and that it is what will make my translation of the poem differ from those of other translators. So, I have attempted to capture the poet's whimsy. A poem like this wasn't written drunk . . . but the poet would like you to think so, I think.

IV: The last poem of this set is constructed almost entirely of allusions. They are mainly designed to mock Confucian and Taoist philosophies and those who follow them. Buddhists, who are supposed to abstain entirely from wine, are rewarded with silence. Li Po's an iconoclast. The Taoist Chuang Tzu, a witty iconoclast himself, is alluded to in lines 3, 7, 8, 9, and 14 of the original Chinese, at the very least. The reference to Confucius's favorite disciple, Yen Hui, is linked to *both* the *Analects of Confucius* and chapter 6 of the *Chuang Tzu* book. Neither Lao Tzu nor Chuang Tzu comes up, as Li Po does, with wine as *the universal solvent* for the world's problems. Confucius takes the hardest knocks, of course, maybe because in the *Analects of Confucius* the Master never mentions wine. When Li Po chooses to use the character for the word "heap" in the description of the Taoist fairyland, it's probably because it's a character which is also used for Confucius's personal name, Ch'iu. Ch'u Yuan, confusingly seen as both Confucian sage and Taoist alchemist, is alluded to only through the crabs (and shrimp) that skeptics throughout Chinese tradition mention as the beneficiaries of his noble protest suicide by drowning in the Hsiang River. Devout Confucians see his disappearance as a noble exclamation point to the sentence of his loyal protest. Li Po's poem is, in any case, a tour de force of iconoclastic wit.

Looking in the Mirror and Writing What My Heart Finds There (page 97)

See the appendix following these notes for a lengthy elaboration of this one, with word-for-word translation and Chinese characters.

Again, It Weighs Heavily upon My Heart (page 98)

This poem opens with a character that usually "means" simply to desire, to want to, or even to be going to (do something), but which is also the word chosen by the Chinese translators of Buddhist sacred texts from Sanskrit to represent the word *rajas* (passion) or *kama* (sensual desire), both of which are considered obstacles in Buddhism since they bind us by perpetual reincarnation into a lifetime of suffering. The visual similarity of this character to the first character of the last line of the poem, which has strong connotations of stopping or ending, helps the reader of the original to see that the poet has perhaps at last (in this third of three poems on the death of his patron Ho Chih-chang; the first two aren't included here) begun to be able to overcome the desire to have his friend back, the "normal" desire to overcome change itself. This may be true enlightenment. It certainly leads toward enlightenment according to the Buddha.

I Looked All Over the Mountain for the Monk, but Not Finding Him, I Wrote This (page 99)

Many a T'ang poet wrote a poem, or more than one, about looking for a teacher, Taoist or Buddhist, on a mountaintop. It was, to put it gently, simply something one did, or a conventional topic for a poem. But, on the one hand, many Buddhist monks made excellent educated conversation, and occasionally the journey toward a deeper commitment or a deeper understanding began from such a visit. Still, judging from the number of poems of the type that, like this one, include the absence of the monk sought, it looks almost as if poets and monks may often have cooperated to make sure that the monk wouldn't be there to be bothered by a social call, and the poet could get credit, through the work done on the poem, for his long walk in the mountains without having to endure a religious lecture. Often the occasion for a poem was sufficient for the poet. Though the title of this poem seems to imply something similar, in the end, what Li Po recorded (or maybe created) is a much deeper experience than what is offered in the conventional "failing to meet the master" poem.

The poem begins, in the original characters, with four that prominently display *gates*, or doorways, before the poet even reaches the monk's dwelling place. Even nature is closed against *this* seeker, maybe because he's not (yet) sincerely seeking. The last "gate" character is the door of the monk's dwelling or meditation chamber. The poet dares to peek inside, curious and disrespectful as a child.

The construction of the lines conspires to keep us from seeing clearly. The monk is *not* there for *us*. *I'm* forced to interpret: I see that the monk has been gone quite a while. How long does it take dust to settle inside a room on a mountainside? Has he gone for supplies? Does he still live in "this world"? Perhaps he's even died. News traveled slowly in the 700s. The poet's at a loss too; he sighs, and goes round and round and round at length about life and death, about leaving *samsara*, quitting the "round and round." Then he experiences the beauty of *this* world, and wavers. As is often the case in Li Po's poetry, the wailing gibbons play the part of humanity, reminding him about both the warmth and the silliness of primate lives . . . Monkey business. Here, they enter, wailing. It is *so* obvious that he should leave the world. And

then the last line, "Here, this Way? I worry . . ."
I'm sure the poet intended that his eighth-century readers should feel his ambivalence, should feel that his visit to the monk was a true spiritual quest and not a conventional poetic exercise. I felt blessed to have been able to find myself once or twice walking beside the poet in his poem as he walked uphill among the beauties on that mountainside, and to realize that he was giving me the same choice he's been giving himself.

VISITING THE TAO MASTER OF TAI-T'IEN
MOUNTAIN WHEN HE WASN'T THERE
(PAGE 101)

Lao Tzu's Utopian village, in poem 80 of the *Tao Te Ching*, comes to mind in the voices of the dogs and the chickens that are its guards. That leads the way to T'ao Ch'ien's, with a little help from the peach blossoms, which are a guide toward the little village of the Utopia of his "Peach Blossom Spring."

SITTING AT REVERENCE MOUNTAIN (PAGE 102)

At first there is a man sitting in meditation and a mountain called Reverence Mountain. Then there is *only* a mountain. Zen—the word "means" meditation— has been born, and borne fruit.

Thoughts of a Quiet Night (page 103)

See the appendix following these notes for a lengthy elaboration of this one, with word-for-word translation and Chinese characters.

Submitted at the Imperial Command, a Poem Written by the Dragon Pool in the Spring Garden While Viewing the Newly Greening Willows and Listening to the Hundreds of New Songs of the First Nightingales (page 107)

I used Shigeyoshi Obata's accurate translation of this poem in college classes for more than twenty years to show the sort of dreck a Court poet was forced to produce on command. It was only after I undertook to translate the poem *myself*, to look closely at the original characters, that I came to appreciate the efforts of Mr. Obata, and to get a sense of the joy of craftsmanship that Li Po took in the creation of this lively description of the rituals and performances associated with the greeting of Spring, and perhaps of the Spring's new crop of performers from the Pear Garden, the training institute for singers and dancers established early in the reign of the Emperor, when Hsuan Tsung still deserved his popular title, Ming Huang, the Brilliant Emperor. I hope my translation may transmit at least a bit of the excitement I felt in discovering Li Po's art here. Certainly this poem comes pretty close to the boundary of what I suggested in the introduction might be called protest poems. Clearly the poet is awed by his task. On the other hand, there might be just a hint in the wordiness of the title of hidden mockery of the pomp of the Court. Of course it's also possible that long titles were required by court ceremony.

A Song of Bathing (page 110)

The title of the poem refers, I think, to the preparation of the Court officer to make himself ready to be presented at Court before his Lord and Master. The subject of the poem is Li Po himself, figured as Ch'u Yuan, the first non-anonymous poet in China. When his advice, against cooperation with the eventually victorious State of Ch'in, was disregarded and he himself disgraced, he is said to have gone to the Hsiang River, either to seek the Elixir of Immortality with "Taoist" alchemists, or (making himself a hero of Confucians) to prove the selflessness of his advice by drowning himself there. The cap and gown are emblems of government service to the state (and the people), the lifelong goal of the Confucian. The fisherman of Ts'ang-lang is the Taoist who warns of the fruitlessness of such *untimely* idealism.

WAR SOUTH OF THE WALL (PAGE 114)

It's not clear here how much the poet has really seen of war. There is not much "new" in the poem, relative to the Chinese poetic tradition. Study of Lao Tzu would incline Li Po to despise martial "virtues," even if he'd ever really been a knight-errant. What was to come in China would bring Li Po something new: real contact with mass warfare and the rape and pillage that follow it.

The second poem on war appears to me to have been written after some real experience.

A SONG OF FAREWELL AT RED CLIFF (PAGE 116)

The last two lines are purest sarcasm. Allusions to the *Lao Tzu* in lines 2, 6, and 7 of the translation should make it clear that the poem is strongly pacifist. During most of Li Po's adult life, T'ang *ideology* was based on Taoist principles. Modern readers, and moviegoers, will recognize the heroic Chou Yu as the warrior given responsibility in both folklore and official history for saving Chinese civilization from the evil Ts'ao Ts'ao at the battle of Red Cliff. During Li Po's lifetime a serious intellectual battle was taking place, attempting to stop what was seen in many quarters as a militarization of the culture, with Chou Yu as the *antagonist* of the pacifist tradition. The poem seems to me to be a powerful, heartfelt embrace of Taoist pacifism. Our poet may or may not have been a knight-errant in his youth, but he did also without a doubt study at length with several Taoist masters, and the classic master Chuang Tzu and the lay Taoist hero T'ao Ch'ien were certainly the figures most often and most effectively alluded to in his poetic work throughout his life. All were pure pacifists . . . though ruling out neither self-defense nor preparedness.

JADE STAIRS LAMENT (PAGE 119)

In the cut-crystal hangings beside her windows, she is mocked in private, secretly mocked by her lover. Just as in the famous quatrain "Thoughts of a Quiet Night" (page 103; see also the appendix), the moon connects lovers or reminds them of separation (because it is always present at the same *time* in places as far apart as one could be in the *human* past); and in that crystal, the mockery of the moon was repeated again and again. Ezra Pound's ecstatic experience of this poem led directly to the beginning of "Imagism" and thereby, for better or worse, to the creation of a new kind of poetry in America.

THE KING OF WU'S FAVORITE, JUST A LITTLE DRUNK (PAGE 120)

Hsi-shih was one of the many famous Helen of Troy figures of early Chinese history. The King's infatuation with her is held responsible for the fall of his state.

SONG FOR SENG KA (PAGE 123)

A classic Chinese reference work, *The Biographical Dictionary of Chinese Monks* states that Seng Ka died in 710 C.E., when Li Po was only nine years of age. This monk was celebrated among ordinary people in T'ang China, most of all for his magical feats. He was sometimes believed to be a reincarnation of Kuan-yin, the Goddess (or God) of Mercy. *Li Po*'s Seng Ka is a good old-fashioned "spirit," maybe not quite a mere ghost, but pretty near. Without getting into the number and special qualities of the *hun* and the *p'o*, the two kinds of Chinese "souls," nor, in fact, into the relationships between "souls" and "reincarnations" in the Buddhist afterlife, you can see legends, lore, and spiritual knowledge of both the common folk and the educated kind displayed here. How "serious" the poet is in his appreciation of the magician-monk we can only wonder. The poem is called a "song" because it is constructed of lines of uneven lengths, fourteen of seven characters each, and four of three each. In translation, the economy possible in Chinese often mocks the translator's best efforts. Here, where the exuberant language of popular Buddhism invites the poet's imagination to find rivers of sand describing the multiplication of universes (not that such exuberance isn't a feature of elite Buddhist philosophy, and modern Western-style "cosmology," as well), the translator has probably committed a few excesses of his own. "Three Coils" is a translation of the term meaning the three main divisions of the great library of Buddhist thought. I assume that the "Monkey" referred to here is an early reference to the legendary "Monkey King." The presence of the staff seems to support the identification. See David Kherdian's *Monkey: A Journey to the West* (Boston: Shambhala, 2005).

A Pa Girl's Song (PAGE 125)

Pa is an old name for part of Sichuan, where Li Po may have lived a good part of his youth. I find this an almost perfectly sympathetic picture of the simplicity of provincial life and consciousness. The young woman is awed by the speed of the river in spate, and her excitement is expressed in her inability to comprehend concepts of time and space raised by speeds beyond foot step or ox plod. I place it among the protest poems only because it could very well be a precursor of the two Ch'ang-kan poems that follow it. A young poet's poems are often the seeds of his more mature ones: "The child is father to the man."

Ballad of Ch'ang-kan (page 126)

Li Po may be speaking to one of his own wives in the Ch'ang-kan poems, wishing for her both the humility and the courage shown by his ideal creation. Few scholars believe so. As for separation, or physical danger, the wives of river merchants and of the honest officials of the sort Li Po may truly have longed to be may not have differed all that much. Certainly, while the wife of the poem or poems suffers from her life, it is the suffering of a loving wife. She is also clearly proud of her knowledge of the river and its weathers, and I think it is implied, of her knowledge of the family business as well. Paradoxically, perhaps, women of the land-owning "yeomanry" and wives of small businessmen like merchants and craftsmen, even women of the lower peasant class, who made important contributions to the family economy, probably were granted more dignity within the family than all but the luckiest of upper-class women—those *allowed* to be educated by liberal parents.

Passing the Night at the Foot of Five-Pines Mountain in the House of the Widow Ao (page 130)

This poem is a more direct piece of political protest than we usually find among the poems of Li Po's works translated to date. Li Po might be quite sure that this verse will "immortalize" the widow Ao, and also that she may starve before Spring for lack of the meager meal she has shared. An allusion in the next-to-last line links the poem to the story of Han Hsin (d. 196 B.C.E.), who repaid similar generosity after he rose in the world.

Overnight at Shrimp Lake (page 133)

This woodcutter seems like a real person, not a stereotypical "Taoist" woodcutter or fisherman, whose company poets other than Li Po seem to prefer to that of ordinary folks, or other poets.

Omei Mountain Moon (page 137)

Many believe that this poem is an early one. I believe it may contain the first reference to his lifelong friend Meng Hao-jan (689–740 C.E.). This relationship was a profound one, and the metaphorical separation of the boat, which leaves on the river of life, and the mountain staying behind is, to me, profound: profound enough to refer even, perhaps long after the fact, to the separation caused by Meng's death.

AFTER THE ANCIENTS (PAGE 143)

Autumn water has several connotations. Streams that are always muddy in spring are usually low and therefore clear in Autumn in North China, where Chinese poetry began, and so, when a poet refers to a women's eyes, Autumn water often means that they are *clear*.

A SONG OF WHITE CLOUDS: FAREWELL TO A FRIEND (PAGE 144)

Li Po appears to me to be advising a younger associate against the wondering life he has chosen for himself. It is not hard to imagine fifty reasons for such advice, no? The *lady tresses* mentioned are a lichen similar in appearance to the Spanish moss.

IN THE OLD STYLE: I GOT TO THE ISLET BENEATH WU-SHAN (PAGE 146)

See also the poem "By the Riverside, Seeing Off the Lady Master of the Tao" (page 65). Legends involving Wu-shan (Mount Wu, translated as Shamaness Mountain or Witch Mountain), and its shamaness, spirit woman, or spirit-of-the-female, have been around since at least the late Chou period. The Wu herself probably gets her name from the priestesses of the Ch'u State, whose trance-inducing dances allowed them intercourse with the gods, at least. Words or phrases such as "Yang Tower," like "clouds-and-rain" and even "Wu-shan" itself (anytime it seems strangely out of context to have a mountain pop up), are *always* direct indicators of sexual activity in the line of the poem where the term appears. Thus, for instance, this poem involves sex in the opening line and elsewhere, and rumination upon it thereafter.

Climbing the Peak of Great White (page 147)

Since "Great White" is one of Li Po's nicknames, as well as quite possibly the name of a hill to the west of Ch'ang An, and also the name of the morning star (the planet we know as Venus), the poet is talking to himself.

Over Heaven's Old Mama's Mountain in a Dream, at a Farewell Party (page 148)

The title of this poem indicates, surprisingly, that it was written as a "parting poem." I wonder if reference to Taoist *hsien*, or Immortals, likening them to hemp (cannabis) plants standing in rows indicates a place for them in the parting ceremonial. Mao Shan Taoist ceremony used cannabis as "incense" in their "church" ceremonials. The imaginative qualities of this poem, like those of several of the Old

Style poems, are quite different from the already very individual imaginative style exhibited by Li Po. But we must remember that for all its many strictures, T'ang China did not subject an artist's exploration of his own consciousness to legal sanctions . . . nature took care of the overly fearless among the explorers. The free market was *allowed to take its course in punishing irrational exuberance.* The title and the body of the poem have been adjusted by commentators to give the Old Mama a slightly more dignified title, but, taking the peasant voice of the opening lines as Li Po's true narrator, I have gone, or stayed, "down home" for the "location."

OVERNIGHT WITH THE MASTER OF CLEAR CREEK HOUSE (PAGE 151)

This poem ends with what appears to be a "pure phonetic" character, meaning one that's to be read for its sound *only*. This type of character is created by simply adding a single "mouth" element (□) to the left side of the character. Here we get □ + 秋 (mouth + Autumn or Fall) = 啾, the phonetic character that makes a noise like *fall*, and has *no* meaning. Li Po's suggesting that the apes tried to speak. The left-side element in a phonetic character is reduced in size. Li Po wasn't really creating a neologism here. The same phonetic character, and the eye-to-meaning play that arises from it, was first created and used in Ch'u Yuan's famous poem "On Encountering Sorrow" more than a thousand years before Li Po used it here. I hope that doesn't make my addition to the English of apparent surprise on Li Po's part seem disingenuous. The visual pun just seems the *most* interesting part of this otherwise nice little poem, and anything that could re-create its effect for the English reader seemed a reasonable translator's cheat. I hope it made something that was easy and clear to the original reader easy and clear for you.

Ballad of the Voyager (page 153)

Several of Li Po's travel poems are, like this one, perhaps more than anything else, celebrations of the *courage* required of the traveler when what might be an hour's drive today would have been a day or two on foot or horseback, with rivers to cross and rapids to ride and bandits too often waiting in the brush. Li Po's "Down to Chiang-ling" (page 138) expresses this feeling, one compounded of amazement and pride.

In the Old Style: Westward over Lotus Mountain (page 155)

The violent wrenching of time and place, including travel to otherworldly times and places, seems to me to link this poem to the wild travels in the "'Over Heaven's Old Mama's Mountain in a Dream, at a Farewell Party" poem (page 148), and I wonder if the poet may not have been experimenting with drugs other than his beloved alcohol. Mushrooms and ergot (a fungus found on certain grains) were not unknown to particularly "Taoist" spiritual searchers in China. I haven't been able to identify Wei Shu-ch'ing.

Fall Cove Songs (page 157)

I believe that the "Fall Cove Songs" may well have been written at many different times, maybe first when Li Po was practically in hiding after his disgrace at court, and later when he was just resting from his constant search for a comfortable relationship with a wealthy patron. I believe that Fall Cove was one of the small anchorages formed by the many tributaries to Nest Lake (Ch'ao Hu), a large lake that was close to T'ao Ch'ien's home territory in modern Anhui Province.

VII: I take the reference to the Mountain Lord to come from Li Po's own "Hsiang-yang Verses." Ning Chi, the white stones, and the sable coat are all allusions to legends involving poverty and the often, usually near miraculous, attainment of wealth and high position.

XI: The point here is, I think, that in actuality Fall Cove's not pristine (there are smelters in poem XIV), but that beauty is, after all, where you find it, even as other features of a pristine environment disappear.

XIII: The character *su* ("pure" or "white") appears, describing the outstretched hand of a chaste yet abandoned wife, in poem three of the well-known (in China) Nineteen Old Poems of the Han, the poem which was clearly the poet's model for the strange poem XIII of this set. I have supplied the "hand" for you, from that source, which all Li Po's original readers certainly knew by heart.

XV: A cubit, about 18 inches, is far smaller than a *chang* (10 feet), but the purpose of both is just to put a gloss of specificity to a silly, simply unbelievable length. The poem is a cute joke, a little *self*-mockery in the face of aging, but it also helps us see that the *set* of poems is meant to be seen as a brief recap of a lifetime.

XVI: At some point, plumage of the silver pheasant was worn as a badge of an Imperial Officer of the fifth rank, a big deal. This may have been a super-subtle poem. If there is a political level we probably can't reach it, but it might be interesting to think about the possibilities.

Appendix

In this appendix, I analyze two poems: the eight-line poem called "Looking in the Mirror and Writing What My Heart Finds There," and the most famous of all Li Po's quatrains, "Thoughts of a Quiet Night." For each of these I present the Chinese characters of the original poem, followed by a word-for-word translation (WFW), and then by something I'll call simply an "Englished" version, where enough of the pronouns and basic grammar are added to make the WFW understandable for the English reader. For the quatrain I have several times not felt comfortable showing just one line of "Englishing," but have rather added on as many as two more versions of "Englished" lines, each I hope explaining a new level of meaning, and finally achieving the fluency of natural spoken English, though not the beauty and elegant simplicity that hopefully will appear in a completed *poetic* translation.

These second-level word-for-word and "Englished" lines offered at the beginning of the analysis of each poem are what John Dryden, the first great English translator and writer on translation, would, I think, call *metaphrase*: turning an author's work, word by word and line by line, into the language of another. In translation, the translator moves from metaphrase to what Dryden defines as *paraphrase*, "translation with latitude, where the author is kept in view of the translator, so as never to be lost, but his words are not so strictly followed as his *sense*, and that too is admitted to be amplified, but not altered" (emphasis mine). As if this weren't a complex enough task, the pictorial and ideographic nature of the Chinese written characters adds another layer to the translator's job, allowing many of the words to carry multiple direct meanings and many oblique suggestions as well.

In the analysis of these two poems I have replaced the paraphrase stage with a short essay about the forces at work in the original, and how they might influence a translator's decisions in the paraphrasing, or translation, process. When you've studied it all I'll invite you to make your own translation, or to simply take a look at my finished product.

Looking in the Mirror and Writing What My Heart Finds There

覽鏡書懷

得道無古今。
失道還衰老。
自笑鏡中人。
白髮如霜草。
捫心空嘆息。
問影何枯槁。
桃李竟何言。
終成南山皓。

This is a sweet poem, one that I think is able to yield significant meaning at many levels while providing every serious reader an enjoyable experience in the recognition of its brilliant exploitation of language alone. I know from the experience gained in the process of translating and editing a dozen or so other books of Chinese literature that the audience for this book includes both a few people who know Chinese, even Classical Chinese, pretty well, and on the other hand a few people approaching Chinese poetry for the first time. So, as I suggested above, I've started with a word-for-word, and worked my way toward something that might even enable you to have a go at making your own translation. I'd love to discuss your efforts with you at http://poetryeast.com/.

Here's the word-for-word analysis of the first poem:

Title: 覽 鏡 書 懷
WFW: look at | mirror | write | deeply felt
Englished: Writing about what I feel deeply
when I look in the mirror

Line 1: 得 道 無 古 今 。
WFW: get | Tao | there is no | ancient | modern
Englished: Get the Tao and there is no "now" or "then."

If one attains the Tao, one may recover or accomplish a Golden Age, (there will be no difference between then and now), regaining an ancient Paradise like the Eden of the "religions of the book." In this particular poem, it also seems likely that Li Po, who in early life was interested in the possibility of achieving physical immortality through Taoist alchemical practices, is already laughing at himself for that delusion, which he abandoned in later life.

As for the "meaning" of the term *Tao* itself, we'd best leave it "untranslated," since Lao Tzu, the legendary author of Taoism's first and most revered scripture, the *Tao Te Ching*, warns his followers over and over again against attempting to express its meaning in words. As a word in common speech, and this may be very helpful, the word *Tao* means "to go," "a road," "a way of getting from one place to another," or, perhaps strangely, "to speak" (which is, metaphorically at least, *one* way of limping from one place in life to another). The effort to define the central terms of this school of thought is something you can play at very productively without knowing Chinese. Simply gather up four or five of the best-known English translations and pay particular attention both to where they agree and where they don't. You'll at least go a long way toward understanding why both Li Po and his Emperor felt it worthwhile and even necessary to study with a trained master and to take a supervised examination over the contents of the 5,000-word, 81-passage "booklet."

But to get back to line 1 of the poem: "Understand the Way and there is no ancient or modern." It doesn't mean that you are capable of time travel, but it does mean that one aware of the way the "world" works knows that the reins of power, or the ultimate authority over one's own life, is in one's own hands. Note that the *Tao Te Ching* is not a book of "philosophy" in modern terms, but a "wisdom book," and if you understand its message, you'll find it wise. The terror for any translator lies in the feeling of perhaps misleading his or her readers. But we have a poem to deal with here, not the wisdom book itself.

Line 2: 失 道 還 衰 老 。
WFW: lose | Tao | return | wither | (get) old
Englished: Lose the Tao and there's still
     withering old age.

In line 1 we found that to get the Tao is to get all we need. If, on the other hand, you fail to find the Way to function effectively in life, or even to deal with your own feelings of failure, or your fear of death, *still*, still coming at you is that which you wished to control, that which you feared. The first time you read this line you may feel you've found a Li Po you haven't seen elsewhere, a rough man, even a bully. But if he is speaking to himself, and only letting us listen in, he becomes less of a bully, more like a guide, especially if we remember that one issue for him (one that isn't likely, at least not in exactly this form, to be one for us) had been the pursuit of physical immortality through "Taoist" alchemy.

Alchemy was not originally Taoist. It's not directly mentioned by Lao Tzu or his most important "disciple," Chuang Tzu, but it had become tightly linked to Taoism well before Li Po's time. It seems possible, or even likely, that Li Po is mocking his own gullibility. Lao Tzu does not offer "escape" from nature, which includes "old age." If you lose the Tao, you gain *concern* for (or fear of) your own death.

Line 3: 自　笑　鏡　中　人　。
WFW: self (I, me) | laugh, smile, | mirror | in [post-position], | person
 Englished: I laugh at the man in the mirror.

For the rest of the poem Li Po, like a good Taoist, shuts up about the "Tao" (the book says that the one who speaks [about it] does not know) and speaks only about himself, something which, knowing Tao, he may know, I think. He laughs to greet the process of aging because it's one of his oldest acquaintances. He laughs because he is aware of the inevitable reality. The fourth character in line 3 is one you may recognize as a part of the name of China, the Middle Kingdom. Here it is a grammatical word only, a "post-position" (comparable to a "pre-position," but coming after the word it locates rather than, as in English, before it) indicating that the person is "in" the mirror.

Line 4: 白　髮　如　霜　草　。

WFW: white | hair | like | frost | grass
Englished: (My) white hair [is] like frosted grass.
　　　　　Po's hair is white like frosty grass.

Here, what I call a "trick," what literary folks call "poetic technique," is shown in the artistic creation of ambiguity. White is the "color" of frost, but the character is also the *Po* of Li Po's personal name. The *Po* in Li Po's name also means "white." Li Po himself grows white as frost. The mirror "reflects" in more than one way! And it's only the first time Po will work his way into the text of this poem of his.

Line 5:　撚 心 空 嘆息　。
WFW:　　hold | heart-mind | in vain, empty | sigh [2-syllable compound]
Englished: (I) hold the door to (my) heart and vainly sigh.

The character for "hold" consists of a hand, on the left, holding a door or gate, on the right. It is possible that T'ang readers, used to reading characters as pictograms, ideographs, and phonetic compounds, because they were reading the characters as Classical Chinese and not as representatives of the spoken language as people do today, might have seen another character at play here, an invisible character, available from the memory, as it were. A strong word for the concept of melancholy, a feeling we might expect here, is 悶, clearly a compound of 門 "gate" and 心 "heart-and-mind." The Chinese traditionally don't separate the functions of feeling and knowing as we English-speakers do, so the character for heart stands for an organ that does both, and I often translate it "heart-and-mind." Here Li Po holds the door of his heart-and-mind open on the "emptiness" (expressed with the same character as "vanity" in Chinese) and the issues of existence and nonexistence that he must address (and get over also?) if he is to begin exploration of another "way." When *he opens the gate of melancholy thought*, he frees his heart and his mind (his heart-and-mind gets out of the gate that his hand opened) to contemplation of a "Tao" beyond the very limited *Way* that alchemical Taoism offers. A remaining bit of artistry in this line lies in the last two characters. The fourth character, part of the two-syllable compound word for "sighing," is a phonetic containing, on the right, the word *Han*, the Chinese name for themselves (the Chinese) *and* for a manly man. The last character, also a part of the compound word "to sigh," consists of the character for "self" over the character for "heart-and-mind" . . . so Li

Po has neatly claimed that it is manly to sigh so, and he reminds us that it is his own heart-and-mind that insists this.

Line 6:　問　影　何　枯槁　。
WFW:　(I) ask | shadow (reflection) | how | withered [2-syllable compound]
Englished:　I ask shadow how I got like withered wood.

Line 6 as it is "Englished" here is only a little better than a word-for-word translation of the original. It is often necessary to add pronouns to get real English from real Classical Chinese as you've seen; but, in addition, there is an intentional ambiguity about the object of the mirror viewing, the person who is being looked at in the mirror. Does Li Po look at himself reflected from the mirror, or does he see a *shadow* there? The poet suddenly suggests that he may be appealing to his favorite "spiritual guide," T'ao Ch'ien, drinker, philosopher, and at least a peripheral figure, historically, in the Buddhist missionary and translator Hui Yuan's White Lotus Society. This particular *shadow* may well be a figure in a famous poem by T'ao Ch'ien titled "Body, Shadow, Spirit." It's a poem about mortality, and how to approach it. Finding a shadow in the mirror rather than a reflection of the poet may seem far-fetched, but in fact it is just the announcement of the entry of T'ao Ch'ien, via allusions, into the poem.

In the final three lines of Li Po's poem, there are many more allusions, and shared language from T'ao Ch'ien's poetry is interwoven in the poem, making it impossible to move forward in translation from line 7 on without resorting to something beyond paraphrase. But Classical Chinese, with its characters both visual and phonetic, can, as you've seen by now and will see multiplied in the following lines, simply carry more meaning per syllable than our language, great as it is. So I'll try to stay as close to the original as I can, and give the reader a chance to see the sort of problems a translator sometimes (certainly not always) faces in making an honest rendering of the Chinese poet's work as poetry in English.

Line 7: 桃 李 竟 何 言 。
WFW: Peach | plum | in the end, finally | how | speak
Englished: Peaches and plums [peach + plum = 2-syllable compound for "youth"], in the end, what can (you) say?
"Peaches and plums," as a two-syllable phrase, is

a conventional metaphor for youth in China, and the translator, given room and rhythmic possibilities, may and should slip in that information, unobtrusively in the English, since it is there in the Chinese. But *peaches in blossom* are also the marker for the entrance to the Utopian fairyland created by T'ao Ch'ien in a famous prose piece known to every literate Chinese person of Li Po's acquaintance, and most in our time as well. In addition to being emblems of youth, the two *fruits* can also be markers of *discipleship* (the young follower of the elderly teacher, as T'ao Ch'ien is, three centuries later, Li Po's teacher).

There is yet another artistic trick, also quite evidently hidden here. The word for peach is pronounced *T'ao*, the same as the *T'ao* in *T'ao Ch'ien*, and the plum just happens (pray remember that nothing ever "*just* happens" at word level in a great poet's poem)—the plum *just happens* to be the *Li* of *Li Po*. Mr. Plum is his name, *translated* directly into English, with his given name, Po, meaning "white," of course. The word-for-word translator is left with a still life with two little fruits; the literary translator has to pass on that information and all the rest, all the information, available to the original reader from the *Chinese* word-for-word, but not even hinted at to the English reader peach by peach, and plum by plum.

As a final fillip, the character used here for

"in the end" is the same character as that used for mirror above, with a single element removed. The element removed means "metal" which was the material from which mirrors were constructed (polished bronze most often) in T'ang. The fact that humans are not constructed of metal, and that we are, therefore, concerned about dying, is often mentioned in ancient Chinese poetry, in fact. And, almost of course, there is a pun connecting these two characters too, but (you may be prepared to say thank goodness) it's a little too abstruse to permit interpretation here. But let's away to the final line!

Line 8: 終 成 南山 皓 。
WFW: in the end | become | South Mountain | old, white
Englished: (In) the end, we (I / everyone) become(s) white (bones, skulls?) on South Mountain.

There are eight references to South Mountain in *The Poetry Classic* (*Shih Ching*), six of which deal with death, and two of which suggest the possibility of immortality of some kind. To top it off, T'ao Ch'ien refers to South Mountain in one of his most famous poems, poem V from the poet's set "Drinking Wine: Twenty Verses," where he also ponders death and the possibility of achieving physical immortality through Taoist alchemy. In a final similarity, he also contemplates South Mountain as his last resting place. T'ao Ch'ien was, at the time he wrote his poem, living as an actual farmer working among his laborers, and apparently looking forward to the honorable funeral due a farmer according to the ancient poems of the *Shih Ching;* but, like most educated Chinese, he was famously skeptical about all kinds of *magic.* The drug alcohol and the Confucian counterpart of the *vita apostolica* seem to have been good enough for him. Yet he did more than once tentatively hold the door to his heart open to the great Buddhist translator-teacher Hui Yuan and his White Lotus Society. In the end, apparently he rejected Buddhism, still in his day regarded by many as a foreign religion.

Our poet, the "spirit of poetry incarnate" and the God of Wine, has one last little flourish for us; at first it may seem trivial and yet somehow it feels perfect. If you read Chinese, or look back at the poem's lines, you'll note the presence of the element *Po (Bai,* in the modern pronunciation), or "white," as a part of the *very last* character in the poem. So Li Po has placed his whole name, hidden in plain sight, in the last two lines of the poem. His family name, Li, appears as a plum ripening in a Utopian fairyland, and his given name closes the parenthesis of life as a piece of *whitening skull* on a hillside.

When you encounter my *paraphrase* of this poem on page 97, I hope you will understand, and maybe even appreciate, the homage intended there to the art of Li Po, and to the inspiration given him by his master, T'ao Ch'ien.

Strangely enough, primarily because Classical Chinese and colloquial American English are so similar in vocabulary and grammar, something like what we call metaphrase is actually very often nearly the same as word-for-word. You may have noticed that some of the above "Englished" lines are very close to word-for-word, but also are already well beyond being metaphrases. The similarity in vocabulary comes primarily from the presence of so many single-syllable words in English from its Germanic roots, matched by the single-syllable words in the Classical, poetic version of Chinese, which intentionally does away with the primarily polysyllabic words of spoken Chinese. (Yes, there are actually many more polysyllabic words than monosyllabic ones in modern spoken Chinese, no matter what you've been told!)

In terms of grammar, the similarities of the two languages come mainly from the fact that both Classical Chinese and colloquial English are primarily subject/verb/object languages (though there are many, many exceptions). Thus, there are many lines and some complete poems that can be translated effectively with something that looks a lot like pretty pure metaphrase. Anyone who would like to see a set of poems intentionally rendered from Chinese so far as possible in metaphrase, or word for word, might enjoy a look at my translations attached to François Cheng's truly wonderful *Chinese Poetic Writing,* translated by Donald A. Riggs and J. P. Seaton (Bloomington: Indiana University Press, 1982).

Generally speaking, though, paraphrase is an absolute necessity. As Dryden said, it is vital not to go *beyond* what is in the original, any more than you would intentionally leave something out. And that, for many translators, is just where the rub lies. You can't know how hard the job is until you try it, but I've enjoyed it for nearly fifty years now.

Thoughts of a Quiet Night

靜夜思

床前明月光。
疑是地上霜。
舉頭 望明月。
低頭思故鄉。

Title: 靜 夜 思

WFW: quiet (adj.) | night (n., adj.) |
   thoughts (n.), or think (v.)

Englished: Thoughts of a quiet night

Line 1: 床 前 明 月 光 。

WFW: bed (n.) | in front of [post-position]
   | bright (adj.) | moon (n.) | shines (v.)

Englished: In front of (my) bed bright
   moonlight (shines).

Line 2: 疑 是 地 上 霜 。

WFW: suspect (v.) | is, it is | floor | on
   [post-position], | frost

Englished: I suspected it (was) (frost on the
   ground, or floor).
   or I (falsely) took it to be floor with frost on it.
   or I wrongly thought it [the light] (was
      caused by / came from) frost on the
      floor.

Line 3: 舉 頭 望 明 月 。

WFW: raise (v.) | head (n.) | gaze (v.), hope
   (v.) | bright (adj.) | moon (n.)

Englished: (I) raised (my) head (and) gazed
   (with hope?) (at) the bright moon.
   or I raised my head and (gazed hopefully) at
   the bright moon.

Line 4: 低 頭 思 故 鄉 。

WFW: lower, bow (v.) | head (n.) | think,
    ponder | old, ancient (adj.) | rural,
    countryside (the old place at home, home)

Englished: (I) lowered (bowed?) (my) head
    [and] thought of my old home (pondered
    the place where I was born).

    or I lowered (bowed) my head and thought
    of home.

Take a peek at page 103 for my cowardly "trans-
lation" of this poem. I've never seen an English ver-
sion of this poem, including my own, that deserves
to be called a *translation*. Certainly no translated
version could ever have become the poem known
by more people than any other poem in the history
of the world, with all its cultures and languages.

Maybe you can already tell some of the special
things about this little poem by looking at the orig-
inal Chinese and the word-for-words, but *content* is
also a very great contributor to the greatness of the
poem, as it always is, of every poem, of course. This
poem is *about* being away from home as autumn
approaches. In North China and in the moun-
tainous regions of the West and Central China as
well, frost marks the beginning of Autumn and the
coming of the trials of Winter. It is also, of course,
symbolic of the onset of old age. To die away from

home, among strangers, is to chance being unable to find a place in the family graveyard, and to find only a diminished place in the memorial rites for family. The significance of this content is not nearly so powerful in any modern society as it was in any premodern one. In ours, travel is just too easy. If I'm lonely in Chicago in late Autumn, I can fly home to Sydney in less than a day. It doesn't take a lot of sympathy to understand how powerful the *content* alone *could* have been in another age. But there are some other elements of the poem, elements made possible only by the nature of the Chinese writing system itself, that also account for its impact in the original, on the original audience.

You'll easily note that the first line in the original Chinese has two characters, the first "bright" (明, *ming*) and the "moon" that share the element 月 (*yue*, moon). If you look more closely, to the immediate left of "bright" you'll see a grammatical particle, a "post-position" like the ones you were introduced to above. Look at the lower left side of 前 (*ch'ien*), "in front of, before." Another moon.

The traditional Chinese had a habit of "using" the moon for an imaginative sort of long-distance communication with loved ones. In fact, in traditional times, there existed a "moon-viewing party," at which people sat quietly on moonlit nights, particularly under a full moon, and thought of (or pondered?) loved ones far away, inside the vast reaches of China proper and even overseas, who might themselves be sitting sharing the same moon at the same time, in the same reverent silence. The fact that the moon, whose many reflected images all reflect the same source, is regarded as a symbol of the "Buddha-nature," a shared spirit shining from the same Source as well, surely deepens the sense of togetherness for Buddhist believers.

So again, *content* is at the base of the power of the poem, but the *twice* thrice-repeated (as we'll see) *picture of the moon*, in the word for the moon itself, in the word for "brightness," and then picked up once more from a *mere* bit of grammar, what is for English speakers a mere "preposition," is simply amazing to me. And this, as I already insisted above, is just the first of two such tricks. Just look a little further: in line 3, the third character, the verb 望 that insists that we gaze again at the bright moon, that insists that we raise our gaze with hope toward the moon: *there also* we find the moon peeking (look again at 望, in the upper right-hand quadrant), as if from behind a cloud. . . .

Oh, and there's one more little trick: notice the final character of the title, 思. It reappears in the middle of the final line, line 4. It is not an uncommon character, but here it is again peculiarly powerful in a way that defies direct translation. The character 思 (*ssu*, think, ponder) is, like 明 (*ming*, bright), what is called a compound ideogram. The meaning of *ming* is implied by the interaction of its two pictorial elements, 日 (*r*, the sun) and 月 (*yue*, the moon). Etymologically, *ssu* 思 is a little complicated, but if you're still with me, you'll be glad you stayed: originally, *ssu* had a 首 (*shou*, a standard old pictograph for "head") on top of 心 "heart" (already in the T'ang it had a synonym, the 頭 that appears twice for "head" in this poem), and also, by T'ang times, the 首 had been replaced by a simpler element, close to a look-alike, 田 (*t'ien*, a field, a garden), so as a visual signifier where 思 once clearly showed that its meaning (remember, it's "to think" or "ponder") is what you do with your head and your heart, it now seems to have been de-rived—and isn't it great for Li Po's purposes—from the conjunction of agricultural fields and gardens resting on the "heart-and-mind" . . . to be thinking, as the once immensely popular country song had it, of "the green, green grass of home."

Sorry for the almost technical jargon and the prickly grammatical constructions, but when you're talking about things that only specialist audiences usually talk about, it's hard to find the vocabulary to be clear with. But what's important, if I've finally gotten it across to you, is that this giant of a poet, using the characters for all they are worth, has milked content central to his culture and to the 心 heart-and-mind of nearly everyone in it, for every bit of sentiment possible. With a little navigating at Professor Pei Ming's China the Beautiful website (www.chinapage.com), you can hear the poem being chanted in the traditional style by my late, revered teacher, Prof. Liu Wu-chi (son of Chairman Mao's poetry teacher, Liu Ya-tzu).

I agree wholeheartedly with John Dryden that paraphrase is *necessary* for good translation, but clearly his conception of the paraphrase may often be *not enough* for translation of certain kinds of Chinese poems. I have published several versions of the quatrain "Thoughts of a Quiet Night." I'm proud of them all, and of the one presented in this book, an improvement on all the previous, I hope. I believe it is a good compromise, but compromise never made anything *great* but a *peace*. Luckily, it is very seldom that such a great poem comes so close to losing all sign of the reasons for its greatness when it goes from one language to another. If it were always this hard to make an adequate translation I would surely have given it up a long, long time ago.

Below you'll find a piece I believe is a far *truer* version of Li Po's "Thoughts of a Quiet Night" than any of my others. It is *freer* than any other translation in the book, though there are certainly a few others, some full poems and some single or multiple lines of other poems, whose interpretation may be questioned by specialists. But this one represents for me the sort of translation of Chinese that should be being done by every translator with sufficient knowledge of Chinese to try it. I guess we live in the shadow of Ezra Pound's misunderstanding of Chinese, or our misunderstanding of his. There are plenty of Chinese poems that are practically photographic: these translate beautifully almost word for word, and when we add a little knowledge of Chinese symbolism, with introductions or notes, we have true translations, usually quite "imagistic," that make for good reading. But there are other kinds of poems, poems like the two I've discussed here, that I believe *require* a freer method to become real poems in English. I hope more translators will dare to try to make such translations when they find such poems. As for me, I'm happy, a week before my seventieth birthday, to be letting this Great P'eng bird fly up from that little (seeming) quatrain. At least my heart feels lighter, as Autumn comes on.

Thoughts of a Quiet Night, Version 2

Pool of cold, pure light, bright on the floor
before the bed. "Can it be *frost*," I shivered,
      "*already?*"
Before I realized, twice bright as frost, it was the
      moon's
own light come streaming through the window
made the window's image purest white of
      moonlight
on my floor. I raised up, to *regard* the moon, to
      see it, sure, and
read its meaning: this too will slip away. And
      then I bowed,
I bowed my head, my heart hope filled again,
      full of the bright moonlight
on the green, green grass of home.